Our English Lakes,

MOUNTAINS, AND WATERFALLS,

AS SEEN BY

WILLIAM WORDSWORTH.

1870.

WILLIAM WORDSWORTH

"Mr. Wordsworth . . . had a dignified manner, with a deep and roughish but not unpleasing voice, and an exalted mode of speaking. He had a habit of keeping his left hand in the bosom of his waistcoat; and in this attitude, except when he turned round to take one of the subjects of his criticism from the shelves (for his contemporaries were there also), he sat dealing forth his eloquent but hardly catholic judgments. . . . Walter Scott said that the eyes of Burns were the finest he ever saw. I cannot say the same of Mr. Wordsworth; that is, not in the sense of the beautiful, or even of the profound. But certainly I never beheld eyes which looked so inspired and supernatural. They were like fires half burning, half smouldering with a sort of acrid fixture of regard, and seated at the further end of two caverns. One might imagine Ezekiel or Isaiah to have had such eyes. The finest eyes, in every sense of the word, which I have ever seen in a man's head (and I have seen many fine ones), are those of Thomas Carlyle."—1815.

AN EXCERPT FROM
The Autobiography of Leigh Hunt, 1850
BY LEIGH HUNT

". . . He (Wordsworth) talked well in his way; with veracity, easy brevity, and force, as a wise tradesman would of his tools and workshop,—and as no unwise one could. His voice was good, frank, and sonorous, though practically clear, distinct, and forcible, rather than melodious; the tone of him business-like, sedately confident; no discourtesy, yet no anxiety about being courteous.

A fine wholesome rusticity, fresh as his mountain breezes, sat well on the stalwart veteran, and on all he said and did. You would have said he was a usually taciturn man; glad to unlock himself to audience sympathetic and intelligent when such offered itself.

His face bore marks of much, not always peaceful, meditation; the look of it not bland or benevolent so much as close, impregnable, and hard: a man *multa tacere loquive paratus*, in a world where he had experienced no lack of contradictions as he strode along! The eyes were not very brilliant, but they had a quiet clearness; there was enough of brow, and well-shaped; rather too much of cheek ('horse face' I have heard satirists say); face of squarish shape, and decidedly longish, as I think the head itself was (its 'length' going horizontal); he was large-boned, lean, but still firm-knit, tall, and strong-looking when he stood, a right good old steel-gray figure, with rustic simplicity and dignity about him, and a vivacious strength looking through him which might have suited one of those old steel-gray markgrafs whom Henry the Fowler set up to ward the 'marches' and do battle with the heathen in a stalwart and judicious manner."

An Excerpt from
Reminiscences, 1881
by Thomas Carlyle

"His features were large, and not suddenly expressive; they conveyed little idea of the 'poetic fire' usually associated with brilliant imagination. His eyes were mild and up-looking, his mouth coarse rather than refined, his forehead high rather than broad; but every action seemed considerate, and every look self-possessed, while his voice, low in tone, had that persuasive eloquence which invariably 'moves men.'"—1832.

An Excerpt from
Memories of Great Men. . . , 1871
by Anna Maria Hall

CONTENTS.

Defcriptions of Scenery.

Domeftic Poems.

EXTRACT FROM THE CONCLUSION OF A POEM, COMPOSED UPON LEAVING SCHOOL.

DEAR native regions, I foretell,
From what I feel at this farewell,
That, wherefoe'er my fteps fhall tend,
And whenfoe'er my courfe fhall end,
If in that hour a fingle tie
Survive of local fympathy,
My foul will caft the backward view,
The longing look alone on you.

Thus, when the fun, prepared for reft,
Hath gained the precincts of the weft,
Though his departing radiance fail
To illuminate the hollow vale,
A lingering light he fondly throws
On the dear hills where firft he rofe.

Winandermere.

᪥

AN EVENING WALK.

FAR from my deareſt Friend, 'tis mine to rove
Through bare grey dell, high wood, and paſtoral
    cove;
His wizard courſe where hoary Derwent takes,
Thro' crags and foreſt glooms and opening lakes,
Staying his ſilent waves, to hear the roar
That ſtuns the tremulous cliffs of high Lodore;
Where peace to Graſmere's lonely iſland leads,
To willowy hedge-rows, and to emerald meads:
Leads to her bridge, rude church, and cottaged grounds,
Her rocky ſheepwalks, and her woodland bounds;
Where, boſom'd deep, the ſhy Winander peeps
'Mid cluſtering iſles, and holly-ſprinkled ſteeps:
Where twilight glens endear my Eſthwaite's ſhore,
And memory of departed pleaſures more.

Fair fcenes, erewhile, I taught, a happy child,
The echoes of your rocks my carols wild :
Then did no ebb of cheerfulnefs demand
Sad tides of joy from melancholy's hand,
In youth's wild eye the livelong day was bright,
The fun at morning, and the ftars at night,
Alike, when firft the vales the bittern fills
Or the firft woodcocks roamed the moonlight hills.

In thoughtlefs gaiety I courfed the plain,
And hope itfelf was all I knew of pain ;
For then, even then, the little heart would beat
At times, while young Content forfook her feat,
And wild Impatience, pointing upward, fhowed,
Where, tipp'd with gold, the mountain fummits glowed.
Alas ! the idle tale of man is found
Depicted in the dial's moral round ;
With hope reflection blends her focial rays
To gild the total tablet of his days ;
Yet ftill, the fport of fome malignant power,
He knows but from its fhade the prefent hour.

But why, ungrateful, dwell on idle pain ?
To fhow her yet fome joys to me remain,
Say, will my Friend, with foft affection's car,
The hiftory of a poet's evening hear ?

When, in the fouth, the wan noon, brooding ftill,
Breathed a pale fteam around the glaring hill,
And fhades of deep-embattled clouds were feen,
Spotting the northern cliffs with lights between ;
Gazing the tempting fhades to them denied,
When ftood the fhortened herds amid the tide,
Where from the barren wall's unfheltered end
Long rails into the fhallow lake extend.
When fchool-boys ftretched their length upon the
          green ;
And round the humming elm, a glimmering fcene,
In the brown park, in flocks the troubled deer
Shook the ftill-twinkling tail and glancing ear ;
When horfes in the wall-girt intake ftood,
Unfhaded, eying far below the flood,
Crowded behind the fwain, in mute diftrefs,
With forward neck the clofing gate to prefs —
Then, as I wandered where the huddling rill
Brightens with water-breaks the hollow ghyll,
To where, while thick above the branches clofe,
In dark brown bafon its wild waves repofe,
Inverted fhrubs, and mofs of darkeft green,
Cling from the rocks, with pale wood-weeds between ;
Save that aloft the fubtile funbeams fhine
On withered briars that o'er the crags recline ;
Sole light admitted here, a fmall cafcade,
Illumines with fparkling foam the twilight fhade ;

Beyond, along the vifta of the brook,
Where antique roots its buftling path o'erlook,
The eye repofes on a fecret bridge,
Half grey, half fhagged with ivy to its ridge.

Sweet rill, farewell ! To-morrow's noon again
Shall hide me, wooing long thy wildwood ftrain;
But now the fun has gained his weftern road,
And eve's mild hour invites my fteps abroad.

While, near the midway cliff, the filvered kite
In many a whiftling circle wheels her flight;
Slant watery lights, from parting clouds, apace
Travel along the precipice's bafe :
Cheering its naked wafte of fcattered ftone,
By lichens grey, and fcanty mofs, o'ergrown ;
Where fcarce the foxglove peeps, or thiftle's beard;
And reftlefs ftone-chat all day long is heard.

How pleafant, as the yellowing fun declines,
And with long rays and fhades the landfcape fhines ;
To mark the birches' ftems all golden light,
That lit the dark flant woods with filvery white ;
The willow's weeping trees, that twinkling hoar,
Glanced oft upturned along the breezy fhore,
Low bending o'er the coloured water, fold
Their movelefs boughs and leaves like threads of gold ;

The fkiffs with naked mafts at anchor laid,
Before the boat-houfe peeping through the fhade ;
The unwearied glance of woodman's echoed ftroke ;
And curling from the trees the cottage fmoke.

Their panniered train a group of potters goad,
Winding from fide to fide up the fteep road ;
The peafant, from yon cliff of fearful edge
Shot, down the headlong path darts with his fledge ;
Bright beams the lonely mountain-horfe illume
Feeding 'mid purple heath, green rings, and broom ;
While the fharp flope the flackened team confounds,
Downward the ponderous timber-wain refounds ;
In foamy breaks the rill, with merry fong,
Dafhed down the rough rock, lightly leaps along ;
From lonefome chapel, at the mountain's feet,
Three humble bells their ruftic chime repeat ;
Sounds from the waterfide the hammered boat ;
And blafted quarry thunders, heard remote!

Even here, amid the fweep of endlefs woods,
Blue pomp of lakes, high cliffs, and falling floods,
Not undelightful are the fimpleft charms,
Found by the graffy door of mountain-farms.

Sweetly ferocious, round his native walks,
Pride of his fifter-wives, the monarch ftalks ;

Spur-clad his nervous feet, and firm his tread ;
A creſt of purple tops his warrior head ;
Bright ſparks his black and rolling eye-ball hurls
Afar, his tail he cloſes and unfurls ;
On tiptoe reared, he ſtrains his clarion throat,
Threatened by faintly-anſwering farms remote.

Bright'ning the cliffs between where ſombrous pine
And yew-trees o'er the ſilver rocks recline ;
I love to mark the quarry's moving trains,
Dwarf panniered ſteeds, and men, and numerous wains ;
How buſy the enormous hive within,
While Echo dallies with the various din !
Some (hardly heard their chiſels' clinking ſound)
Toil, ſmall as pigmies in the gulf profound ;
Some, dim between th' aërial cliffs deſcried,
O'erwalk the ſlender plank from ſide to ſide ;
Theſe, by the pale-blue rocks that ceaſeleſs ring,
Glad from their airy baſkets hang, and ſing.

Hung o'er a cloud above the ſteep that rears
Its edge all flame, the broadening ſun appears ;
A long blue bar its ægis orb divides,
And breaks the ſpreading of its golden tides ;
And now it touches on the purple ſteep
That flings his ſhadow on the pictured deep.

'Cross the calm lake's blue shades the cliffs aspire,
With towers and woods, a " prospect all on fire ; "
The coves and secret hollows, through a ray
Of fainter gold, a purple gleam betray.
The gilded turf arrays in richer green
Each speck of lawn the broken rocks between,
Deep yellow beams the scattered boles illume,
Far in the level forest's central gloom.
Waving his hat, the shepherd, in the vale,
Directs his winding dog the cliffs to scale,—
That barking, busy, 'mid the glittering rocks,
Hunts, where he points, the intercepted flocks.
Where oaks o'erhang the road the radiance shoots
On tawny earth, wild weeds, and twisted roots :
The druid-stones their lighted fane unfold ;
And all the babbling brooks are liquid gold ;
Sunk to a curve, the day-star lessens still,
Gives one bright glance, and drops behind the hill.

In these lone vales, if aught of faith may claim,
Their silver hairs, and ancient hamlet fame,
When up the hills, as now, retreats the light,
Strange apparitions mock the village sight.

A desperate form appears, that spurs his steed
Along the midway cliffs with violent speed ;

Unhurt purfues his lengthened flight, while all
Attend, at every ftretch, his headlong fall.
Anon, in order mounts, a gorgeous fhow
Of horfemen-fhadows moving to and fro ;
And now the van is gilt with evening's beam ;
The rear through iron brown betrays a fullen gleam,
While filent ftands the admiring crowd below,
Loft gradual o'er the heights in pomp they go,
Till, but the lonely beacon, all is fled
That tips with eve's lateft gleam his fpiry head.

Now, while the folemn evening fhadows fail,
On red flow-waving pinions, down the vale ;
How pleafant near the tranquil lake to ftray,
Where winds the road along a fecret bay,
In all the majefty of eafe divides,
And glorying looks around the filent tides ;
Along the " wild meandering fhore " to view,
Obfequious grace the winding fwan purfue ;
He fwells his lifted cheft and backward flings
His bridling neck between his tow'ring wings ;
On as he floats, the filvered waters glow,
Proud of the varying arch and movelefs form of fnow,
While tender cares and mild domeftic loves
With furtive watch purfue her as fhe moves,
The female with a meeker charm fucceeds,
And her brown little-ones around her leads,

Nibbling the water lilies as they pafs,
Or playing wanton with the floating grafs.
She, in a mother's care, her beauty's pride
Forgets, unwearied watching every fide ;
Alternately they mount her back, and reft
Clofe by her mantling wings' embraces preft.

   Long may they roam thefe hermit waves, that fleep
In birch-befprinkled cliffs embofomed deep,
Thefe fairy holms untrodden, ftill, and green,
Whofe fhades protect the hidden wave ferene,
Whence fragrance fcents the water's defert gale,
The violet and lily of the vale !
Where, though her far-off twilight ditty fteal,
They not the trip of harmlefs milk-maid feel ;
Yon tuft conceals their home, their cottage bower ;
Frefh water-rufhes ftrew the verdant floor ;
Long grafs and willows form the woven wall,
And fwings above the roof the poplar tall.
Thence iffuing oft unwieldy as they ftalk,
They crufh with broad black feet their flowery walk ;
Safe from your door ye hear at breezy morn
The hound, the horfe's tread, and mellow horn ;
No ruder found your defert haunts invades
Than waters dafhing wild, or rocking fhades,
Ye ne'er, like haplefs human wanderers, throw
Your young on winter's winding-fheet of fnow.

Fair Swan ! by all a mother's joys careffed,
Haply fome wretch has eyed, and called thee
    bleffed ;
I fee her now, denied to lay her head,
On cold blue nights, in hut or ftraw-built fhed,
Turn to a filent fmile their fleepy cry,
By pointing to a fhooting ftar on high.
—When low-hung clouds each ftar of fummer hide,
And firelefs are the valleys far and wide,
Where the brook brawls along the public road
Dark with bat-haunted afhes ftretching broad,
Oft has fhe taught them on her lap to play
Delighted with the glowworm's harmlefs ray,
Tofs light from hand to hand, while on the ground
Small circles of green radiance gleam around.

Oh ! when the bitter fhowers her path affail,
And roars between the hills the torrent gale ;
No more her breath can thaw their fingers cold,
Their frozen arms her neck no more can fold ;
Weak roof a cowering form two babes to fhield,
And faint the fire a dying heart can yield !
Prefs the fad kifs, fond mother ! vainly fears
Thy flooded cheek to wet them with its tears ;
No tears can chill them, and no bofom warms,
Thy breaft their death-bed, coffined in thine arms !

Sweet are the founds that mingle from afar,
Heard by calm lakes, as peeps the folding ftar,
Where the duck dabbles 'mid the ruftling fedge,
And feeding pike ftarts from the water's edge,
Or the fwan ftirs the reeds, his neck and bill
Wetting, that drip upon the water ftill;
And heron, as refounds the trodden fhore,
Shoots upward, darting his long neck before.

Now, with religious awe, the farewell light
Blends with the folemn colouring of night;
'Mid groves of clouds that creft the mountain's brow,
And round the weft's proud lodge their fhadows throw,
Like Una fhining on her gloomy way,
The half-feen form of Twilight roams aftray;
Shedding, through paly loop-holes mild and fmall,
Gleams that upon the lake's ftill bofom fall;
Soft o'er the furface creep thofe luftres pale
Tracking the fitful motions of the gale.
With reftlefs interchange at once the bright
Wins on the fhade, the fhade upon the light.
No favoured eye was e'er allowed to gaze
On lovelier fpectacle in fairy days;
When gentle Spirits urged a fportive chafe,
Brufhing with lucid wands the water's face;
While mufic, ftealing round the glimmering deeps,
Charmed the tall circle of the enchanted fteeps.

—The lights are vanifhed from the watery plains :
No wreck of all the pageantry remains.
Unheeded, night has overcome the vales :
On the dark earth the baffled vifion fails ;
The lateft lingerer of the foreft train,
The lone black fir, forfakes the faded plain ;
Laft evening fight, the cottage fmoke, no more,
Loft in the thickened darknefs, glimmers hoar ;
And, towering from the fullen dark-brown mere,
Like a black wall, the mountain fteeps appear.
—Now o'er the foothed accordant heart we feel
A fympathetic twilight flowly fteal,
And ever, as we fondly mufe, we find
The foft gloom deepening on the tranquil mind.
Stay ! penfive fadly-pleafing vifions, ftay !
Ah no ! as fades the vale, they fade away :
Yet ftill the tender, vacant gloom remains ;
Still the cold cheek its fhuddering tear retains.

The bird, who ceafed, with fading light, to thread
Silent the hedge or fteamy rivulet's bed,
From his grey re-appearing tower fhall foon
Salute with boding note the rifing moon,
Frofting with hoary light the pearly ground,
And pouring deeper blue to Æther's bound ;
And pleafed, her folemn pomp of clouds to fold
In robes of azure, fleecy-white, and gold.

See o'er the eaftern hill, where darknefs broods
O'er all its vanifhed dells, and lawns, and woods ;
Where but a mafs of fhade the fight can trace,
She lifts in filence up her lovely face :
Above the gloomy valley flings her light,
Far to the weftern flopes with hamlets white :
And gives, where woods the chequered upland ftrew,
To the green corn of fummer, autumn's hue.

Thus Hope, firft pouring from her bleffed horn
Her dawn, far lovelier than the moon's own morn,
'Till higher mounted, ftrives in vain to cheer
The weary hills, impervious, blackening near ;
Yet does fhe ftill, undaunted throw the while
On darling fpots remote her tempting fmile.

Even now fhe decks for me a diftant fcene,
(For dark and broad the gulf of time between,)
Gilding that cottage with her fondeft ray,
(Sole bourn, fole wifh, fole objeɛt of my way ;
How fair its lawns and fheltering woods appear ;
How fweet its ftreamlet murmurs in mine ear !)
Where we, my Friend, to happy days fhall rife,
'Till our fmall fhare of hardly-paining fighs
(For fighs will ever trouble human breath)
Creep hufhed into the tranquil breaft of death.

But now the clear bright Moon her zenith gains,
And, rimy without fpeck, extend the plains :
The deepeft cleft the mountain's front difplays
Scarce hides a fhadow from her fearching rays ;
From the dark-blue faint filvery threads divide
The hills, while gleams below the azure tide ;
The fcene is wakened, yet its peace unbroke
By filvered wreaths of quiet charcoal fmoke,
That o'er the ruins of the fallen wood
Steal down the hill, and fpread along the flood.

The fong of mountain-ftreams, unheard by day,
Now hardly heard, beguiles my homeward way.
All air is like the fleeping water, ftill,
Lift'ning the aërial mufic of the hill,
Broke only by the flow clock tolling deep,
Or fhout that wakes the ferry-man from fleep,
The echoed hoof approaching the far fhore,
Soon followed by his hollow parting oar ;
Sound of clofed gate acrofs the water borne,
Hurrying the feeding hare through ruftling corn ;
The tremulous fob of the complaining owl ;
And at long intervals the mill-dog's howl ;
The diftant forge's fwinging thump profound ;
Or yell, in the deep woods, of lonely hound.

BRATHAY CHURCH.

. . . So we defcend, and winding round a rock,
Attain a point that fhowed the valley—ftretched
In length before us ; and, not diftant far,
Upon a rifing ground a grey Church-tower,
Whofe battlements were fcreened by tufted trees.
And towards a cryftal Mere, that lay beyond
Among fteep hills and woods embofomed, flowed
A copious ftream with boldly-winding courfe ;
Here traceable, there hidden—there again
To fight reftored, and glittering in the fun.
On the ftream's bank, and everywhere, appeared
Fair dwellings, fingle, or in focial knots ;
Some fcattered o'er the level, others perched
On the hill-fides, a cheerful quiet fcene,
Now in its morning purity arrayed.

From " The Excurfion," Book V.

THE VALLEY OF WINANDER AND BRATHAY CHURCH.

. . . . . Right acrofs the lake
Our pinnace moves ; then, coafting creek and bay,
Glades we beheld, and into thickets peeped,

D

Where couch the fpotted deer; or raifed our eyes
To fhaggy fteeps on which the carelefs goat
Browfed by the fide of dafhing waterfalls;
Thus did the bark, meandering with the fhore,
Purfue her voyage, till a point was gained
Where a projecting line of rock, that framed
A natural pier, invited us to land.

Alert to follow as the Paftor led,
We clomb a green hill's fide; and thence obtained
Slowly, a lefs and lefs obftructed fight
Of the flat meadows and indented coaft
Of the whole lake, in compafs feen : far off
And yet confpicuous, ftood the old Church-tower,
In majefty prefiding o'er the vale
And all her dwellings; feemingly preferved
From the intrufion of a reftlefs world
By rocks impaffable and mountains huge.

Soft heath this elevated fpot fupplied,
With refting-place of moffy ftone; and there
We fate reclined; admiring quietly
The frame and general afpect of the fcene;
And each not feldom eager to make known
His own difcoveries; or to favourite points
Directing notice, merely from a wifh
To impart a joy, imperfect while unfhared.

That rapturous moment ne'er fhall I forget,
When thefe particular interefts were effaced
From every mind !—already had the fun,
Sinking with lefs than ordinary ftate,
Attained his weftern bound ; but rays of light—
Now fuddenly diverging from the orb
Retired behind the mountain tops or veiled
By the denfe air—fhot upwards to the crown
Of the blue firmament—aloft, and wide :
And multitudes of little floating clouds,
Pierced through their thin ethereal mould—ere we,
Who faw, of change were confcious—had become
Vivid as fire : clouds feparately poifed,—
Innumerable multitude of forms
Scattered through half the circle of the fky ;
And giving back, and fhedding each on each,
With prodigal communion, the bright hues
Which from the unapparent fount of glory
They had imbibed, and ceafed not to receive,
That which the heavens difplayed, the liquid deep
Repeated ; but with unity fublime !

From " The Excurfion," Book IX.

IMAGE IN THE STREAM.

.   .   .   .   . Forth we went,
And down the valley on the ſtreamlet's bank
Purſued our way, a broken company,
Mute or converſing, ſingle or in pairs.
Thus having reached a bridge, that overarched
The haſty rivulet where it lay becalmed
In a deep pool, by happy chance we ſaw
A two-fold image; on a graſſy bank
A ſnow-white ram, and in the cryſtal flood
Another and the ſame! Moſt beautiful,
On the green turf, with his imperial front
Shaggy and bold, and wreathed horns ſuperb,
The breathing creature ſtood; as beautiful
Beneath him, ſhowed his ſhadowy counterpart.
Each had his glowing mountains, each his ſky,
And each ſeemed centre of his own fair world:
Antipodes unconſcious of each other,
Yet, in partition, with their ſeveral ſpheres,
Blended in perfeᴄt ſtillness to our ſight!

From " The Excurſion," Book IX.

ISLAND ON THE LAKE.

.   .   .   .   Grateful tafk !—to me
Pregnant with recollections of the time
When on thy bofom, fpacious Windermere!
A Youth, I practifed this delightful art;
Toffed on the waves alone, or 'mid a crew
Of joyous comrades. Now the reedy marge
Cleared, with a ftrenuous arm I dipped the oar
Free from obftruction ; and the boat advanced
Through cryftal water, fmoothly as a hawk,
That, difentangled from the fhady boughs
Of fome thick wood, her place of covert, cleaves
With correfponding wings the abyfs of air.
—" Obferve," the Vicar faid, " yon rocky ifle
With birch-trees fringed ; my hand fhall guide the helm,
While thitherward we bend our courfe ; or while
We feek that other, on the weftern fhore,
Where the bare columns of thofe lofty firs,
Supporting gracefully a maffy dome
Of fombre foliage, feem to imitate
A Grecian temple rifing from the Deep."

From " The Excurfion," Book IX.

THERE WAS A BOY.

There was a boy; ye knew him well, ye cliffs
And iflands of Winander! Many a time,
At evening, when the earlieft ftars began
To move along the edges of the hills,
Rifing or fetting, would he ftand alone,
Beneath the trees, or by the glimmering lake ;
And there, with fingers interwoven, both hands
Preff'd clofely palm to palm, and to his mouth
Uplifted, he, as through an inftrument,
Blew mimic hootings to the filent owls,
That they might anfwer him. And they would fhout
Acrofs the watery vale, and fhout again,
Refponfive to his call,—with quivering peals,
And long halloos, and fcreams, and echoes loud
Redoubled and redoubled ; concourfe wild
Of mirth and jocund din! And, when it chanced
That paufes of deep filence mock'd his fkill,
Then, fometimes, in that filence, while he hung
Liftening, a gentle fhock of mild furprife
Has carried far into his heart the voice
Of mountain torrents ; or the vifible fcene

Would enter unawares into his mind
With all its folemn imagery, its rocks,
Its woods, and that uncertain heaven, received
Into the bofom of the fteady lake.

This boy was taken from his mates, and died
In childhood, ere he was full twelve years old.
Fair are the woods, and beauteous is the fpot,
The vale where he was born ; the churchyard hangs
Upon a flope above the village fchool ;
And there, along that bank, when I have paff'd
At evening, I believe that oftentimes
A long half- hour together I have ftood
Mute—looking at the grave in which he lies !

Esthwaite.

LINES

Left upon a Seat in a Yew-Tree, which ſtands near the Lake of Eſthwaite, on a deſolate part of the ſhore commanding a beautiful proſpect.

AY, Traveller! reſt. This lonely Yew-tree ſtands
Far from all human dwelling : what if here
No ſparkling rivulet ſpread the verdant herb ?
What if theſe barren boughs the bee not loves ?
Yet, if the wind breathe ſoft, the curling waves
That break againſt the ſhore, ſhall lull thy mind
By one ſoft impulſe ſaved from vacancy.

Who he was
That piled theſe ſtones, and with the moſſy ſod
Firſt covered o'er, and taught this aged tree
With its dark arms to form a circling bower,
I well remember.—He was one who owned
No common ſoul. In youth by ſcience nurſed,

And led by Nature into a wild fcene
Of lofty hopes, he to the world went forth
A favoured being, knowing no defire
Which genius did not hallow,—'gainft the taint
Of diffolute tongues, and jealoufy, and hate,
And fcorn,—againft all enemies prepared,
All but neglect.   The world, for fo it thought,
Owed him no fervice ; wherefore he at once
With indignation turned himfelf away,
And with the food of pride fuftained his foul
In folitude.—Stranger ! thefe gloomy boughs
Had charms for him ; and here he loved to fit,
His only vifitants a ftraggling fheep,
The ftone-chat, or the fand-lark,
And on thefe barren rocks, with juniper,
And heath and thiftle, thinly fprinkled o'er,
Fixing his downcaft eye, he many an hour
A morbid pleafure nourifhed, tracing here
An emblem of his own unfruitful life :
And lifting up his head, he then would gaze
On the more diftant fcene,—how lovely 'tis
Thou feeft,—and he would gaze till it became
Far lovelier, and his heart could not fuftain
The beauty, ftill more beauteous !   Nor, that time,
When Nature had fubdued him to herfelf,
Would he forget thofe beings, to whofe minds,
Warm from the labours of benevolence,

The world, and man himfelf, appeared a fcene
Of kindred lovelinefs : then he would figh
With mournful joy, to think that others felt
What he muft never feel : and fo, loft Man !
On vifionary views would fancy feed,
Till his eye ftreamed with tears. In this deep vale
He died,—this feat his only monument.

If Thou be one whofe heart the holy forms
Of young imagination have kept pure,
Stranger ! henceforth be warned ; and know that pride,
Howe'er difguifed in his own majefty,
Is littlenefs ; that he who feels contempt
For any living thing, hath faculties
Which he hath never ufed ; that thought with him
Is in its infancy. The man whofe eye
Is ever on himfelf, doth look on one,
The leaft of Nature's works, one who might move
The wife man to that fcorn which wifdom holds
Unlawful, ever. O be wifer, thou !
Inftructed that true knowledge leads to love,
True dignity abides with him alone
Who, in the filent hour of inward thought,
Can ftill fufpect, and ftill revere himfelf,
In lowlinefs of heart.

TO HIS BROTHER.

When, to the attractions of the bufy world,
Preferring ftudious leifure, I had chofen
A habitation in this peaceful vale,
Sharp feafon followed of continual ftorm
In deepeft Winter; and from week to week,
Pathway, and lane, and public road, were clogged
With frequent fhowers of fnow. Upon a hill,
At a fhort diftance from my cottage, ftands
A ftately fir-grove, whither I was wont
To haften, for I found, beneath the roof
Of that perennial fhade, a cloiftral place
Of refuge, with an unincumbered floor.
Here, in fafe covert, on the fhallow fnow,
And fometimes on a fpeck of vifible earth,
The red-breaft near me hopped; nor was I loth
To fympathize with vulgar coppice birds
That, for protection from the nipping blaft,
Hither repaired.—A fingle beech-tree grew
Within this grove of firs; and on the fork
Of that one beech, appeared a thrufh's neft,
A laft year's neft, confpicuoufly built
At fuch fmall elevation from the ground

As gave fure fign that they who in that houfe
Of nature and of love had made their home
Amid the fir-trees all the Summer long,
Dwelt in a tranquil fpot.   And often-times
A few fheep, ftragglers from fome mountain-flock,
Would watch my motions with fufpicious ftare,
From the remoteft outfkirts of the grove,—
Some nook where they had made their final ftand,
Huddling together from two fears—the fear
Of me and of the ftorm.   Full many an hour
Here did I lofe.   But in this grove the trees
Had been fo thickly planted, and had thriven
In fuch perplexed and intricate array,
That vainly did I feek, between their ftems,
A length of open fpace,—where to and fro
My feet might move without concern or care :
And, baffled thus, before the ftorm relaxed,
I ceafed that fhelter to frequent,—and prized,
Lefs than I wifhed to prize, that calm recefs.

     The fnows diffolved, and genial Spring returned
To clothe the fields with verdure.   Other haunts
Meanwhile were mine ; till, one bright April day,
By chance retiring from the glare of noon
To this forfaken covert, there I found
A hoary pathway traced between the trees,
And winding on with fuch an eafy line

Along a natural opening, that I ftood,
Much wondering at my own fimplicity,
How I could e'er have made a fruitlefs fearch
For what was now fo obvious.   At the fight
Conviction alfo flafhed upon my mind
That this fame path (within the fhady grove
Begun and ended) by my Brother's fteps
Had been impreffed.—To fojourn a fhort while
Beneath my roof, he from the barren feas
Had newly come—a cherifhed vifitant !
And much did it delight me to perceive
That to this opportune recefs allured,
He had furveyed it with a finer eye,
A heart more wakeful ; that, more loth to part
From place fo lovely, he had worn the track
By pacing here, unwearied and alone,
In that habitual reftleffnefs of foot
With which the failor meafures o'er and o'er
His fhort domain upon the veffel's deck,
While fhe is travelling through the dreary fea.
When thou hadft quitted Efthwaite's pleafant fhore,
And taken thy firft leave of thofe green hills
And rocks that were the play-ground of thy youth,
Year followed year, my Brother ! and we two,
Converfing not, knew little in what mould
Each other's minds were fafhioned ; and at length,
When once again we met in Grafmere Vale,

Between us there was little other bond
Than common feelings of fraternal love.
But thou, a fchool-boy, to the fea hadft carried
Undying recollections; Nature there
Was with thee; fhe, who loved us both, fhe ftill
Was with thee; and even fo didft thou become
A *filent* poet; from the folitude
Of the vaft fea didft bring a watchful heart
Still couchant, an inevitable ear,
And an eye practifed like a blind man's touch.
Back to the joylefs ocean thou art gone;
And now I call the pathway by thy name,
And love the fir-grove with a perfect love.
Thither do I withdraw when cloudlefs funs
Shine hot, or wind blows troublefome and ftrong:
And there I fit at evening, when the fteep
Of Silver-How, and Grafmere's placid lake
And one green ifland, gleam between the ftems
Of the dark firs, a vifionary fcene!
And, while I gaze upon the fpectacle
Of clouded fplendour, on this dream-like fight
Of folemn lovelinefs, I think on thee,
My Brother, and on all which thou haft loft.
Nor feldom, if I rightly guefs, while thou,
Muttering the verfes which I muttered firft
Among the mountains, through the midnight watch
Art pacing to and fro the veffel's deck

In fome far region, here, while o'er my head,
At every impulfe of the moving breeze,
The fir-grove murmurs with a fea-like found,
Alone I tread this path ;—for aught I know,
Timing my fteps to thine ; and, with a ftore
Of undiftinguifhable fympathies,
Mingling moft earneft wifhes for the day
When we, and others whom we love, fhall meet
A fecond time in Grafmere's happy vale.

Langdale.

BLEA TARN.

THESE ferious words
Clofed the preparatory notices
With which my Fellow-traveller had beguiled
The way, while we advanced up that wide vale.
Now, fuddenly diverging, he began
To climb upon its weftern fide a ridge
Pathlefs and fmooth, a long and fteep afcent,
As if the object of his queft had been
Some fecret of the mountains, cavern, fall
Of water, or fome boaftful eminence
Renowned for fplendid profpect far and wide;
We clomb, without a track to guide our fteps,
And on the fummit reached a heathy plain,
With a tumultuous wafte of huge hill-tops
Before us; favage region! and I walked
In wearinefs: when, all at once, behold!

Beneath our feet, a little lowly vale,
A lowly vale, and yet uplifted high
Among the mountains ; even as if the fpot
Had been from eldeft time by wifh of theirs
So placed, to be fhut out from all the world !
Urn-like it was in fhape, deep as an urn ;
With rocks encompaffed, fave that to the fouth
Was one fmall opening, where a heath-clad ridge
Supplied a boundary lefs abrupt and clofe ;
A quiet, treelefs nook, with two green fields,
A liquid pool that glittered in the fun,
And one bare dwelling ; one abode, no more !
It feemed the home of poverty and toil,
Though not of want : the little fields, made green
By hufbandry of many thrifty years,
Paid cheerful tribute to the moorland houfe.
—There crows the cock, fingle in his domain :
The fmall birds find in fpring no thicket there
To fhroud them ; only from the neighbouring vales
The cuckoo, ftraggling up to the hill-tops,
Shouteth faint tidings of fome gladder place.

Ah ! what a fweet Recefs, thought I, is here !
Inftantly throwing down my limbs at eafe
Upon a bed of heath ;—full many a fpot
Of hidden beauty have I chanced to efpy
Among the mountains ; never one like this ;

F

So lonefome, and fo perfectly fecure ;
Not melancholy—no, for it is green,
And bright, and fertile, furnifhed in itfelf
With the few needful things that life requires.
—In rugged arms how foft it feems to lie,
How tenderly protected ! Far and near
We have an image of the priftine earth,
The planet in its nakednefs : were this
Man's only dwelling, fole appointed feat,
Firft, laft, and fingle, in the breathing world,
It could not be more quiet : peace is here
Or nowhere ; days unruffled by the gale
Of public news or private ; years that pafs
Forgetfully ; uncalled upon to pay
The common penalties of mortal life,
Sicknefs, or accident, or grief, or pain.

From " The Excurfion," Book II.

LANGDALE PIKES.

.   .   .   .   .   In genial mood,
While at our paftoral banquet thus we fate
Fronting the window of that little cell,
I could not, ever and anon, forbear
To glance an upward look on two huge Peaks,
That from fome other vale peered into this.

" Thofe lufty twins, on which your eyes are caft,"
Exclaimed our hoft, " if here you dwelt, would be
Your prized companions.—Many are the notes
Which, in his tuneful courfe, the wind draws forth
From rocks, woods, caverns, heaths, and dafhing fhores ;
And well thofe lofty brethren bear their part
In the wild concert—chiefly when the ftorm
Rides high ; then all the upper air they fill
With roaring found, that ceafes not to flow,
Like fmoke, along the level of the blaft,
In mighty current ; theirs, too, is the fong
Of ftream and headlong flood that feldom fails ;
And, in the grim and breathlefs hour of noon,
Methinks that I have heard them echo back
The thunder's greeting. Nor have nature's laws
Left them ungifted with the power to yield
Mufic of finer tone ; a harmony,
So do I call it, though it be the hand
Of filence, though there be no voice ;—the clouds,
The mift, the fhadows, light of golden funs,
Motions of moonlight, all come thither—touch,
And have an anfwer—thither come, and fhape
A language not unwelcome to fick hearts
And idle fpirits—there the fun himfelf,
At the calm clofe of fummer's longeft day,
Refts his fubftantial orb ; between thofe heights
And on the top of either pinnacle,

More keenly than elfewhere in night's blue vault
Sparkle the ftars, as of their ftation proud.
Thoughts are not busier in the mind of man
Than the mute agents ftirring there."

From " The Excurfion," Book II.

SCENE IN THE VALLEY.

A Humming Bee—a little tinkling rill—
A pair of falcons wheeling on the wing,
In clamorous agitation, round the creft
Of a tall rock, their airy citadel—
By each and all of thefe the penfive ear
Was greeted in the filence that enfued,
When through the cottage-threfhold we had paffed,
And, deep within that lonefome valley, ftood
Once more beneath the concave of a blue
And cloudlefs fky.—Anon exclaimed our hoft,
Triumphantly difperfing with the taunt
The fhade of difcontent which on his brow
Had gathered,—" Ye have left my cell,—but fee
How Nature hems you in with friendly arms !
And by her help ye are my prifoners ftill.
But which way fhall I lead you ?—how contrive,
In fpot fo parfimonioufly endowed,

That the brief hours, which yet remain, may reap
Some recompence of knowledge or delight ? "
So faying, round he looked, as if perplexed ;
And, to remove thofe doubts, my gray-haired Friend
Said—" Shall we take this pathway for our guide ?—
Upward it winds, as if, in Summer heats,
Its line had firft been fafhioned by the flock
Seeking a place of refuge at the root
Of yon black Yew-tree, whofe protruded boughs
Darken the filver bofom of the crag,
From which it draws its meagre fuftenance.
There, in commodious fhelter, may we reft.
Or let us trace this ftreamlet to its fource ;
Feebly it tinkles with an earthy found,
And a few fteps may bring us to the fpot
Where, haply, crowned with flowerets and green herbs,
The mountain infant to the fun comes forth,
Like human life from darknefs."—A fudden turn
Through a ftraight paffage of encumbered ground,
Proved that fuch hope was vain :—for now we ftood
Shut out from profpect of the open vale,
And faw the water that compofed this rill,
Defcending, difembodied, and diffufed
O'er the fmooth furface of an ample crag,
Lofty, and fteep, and naked as a tower.
All further progrefs here was barred ;—And who,
Thought I, if mafter of a vacant hour,

Here would not linger, willingly detained ?
Whether to fuch wild objects he were led
When copious rains have magnified the ftream
Into a loud and white-robed waterfall,
Or introduced at this more quiet time.

   Upon a femicirque of turf-clad ground,
The hidden nook difcovered to our view
A mafs of rock, refembling, as it lay
Right at the foot cf that moift precipice,
A ftranded fhip, with keel upturned, that refts
Fearlefs of winds and waves. Three feveral ftones
Stood near, of fmaller fize, and not unlike
To monumental pillars : and, from thefe
Some little fpace difjoined, a pair were feen,
That with united fhoulders bore aloft
A fragment like an altar, flat and fmooth :
Barren the tablet, yet thereon appeared
A tall and fhining holly that had found
A hofpitable chink, and ftood upright,
As if inferted by fome human hand
In mockery, to wither in the fun,
Or lay its beauty flat before a breeze,
The firft that entered. But no breeze did now
Find entrance ;—high or low appeared no trace
Of motion, fave the water that defcended,
Diffufed adown that barrier of fteep rock,

And foftly creeping like a breath of air,
Such as is fometimes feen, and hardly feen,
To brufh the ftill breaft of a cryftal lake.

From " The Excurfion," Book III.

THE GRANDEUR OF MOUNTAIN SCENERY.

Has not the foul, the being of your life,
Received a fhock of awful confcioufnefs,
In fome calm feafon, when thefe lofty rocks
At night's approach bring down the unclouded fky
To reft upon their circumambient walls ;
A temple framing of dimenfions vaft,
And yet not too enormous for the found
Of human anthems,—choral fong, or burft
Sublime of inftrumental harmony,
To glorify the Eternal !   What if thefe
Did never break the ftillnefs that prevails
Here,—if the folemn nightingale be mute,
And the foft woodlark here did never chant
Her vefpers,—Nature fails not to provide
Impulfe and utterance.   The whifpering air
Sends infpiration from the fhadowy heights
And blind receffes of the caverned rocks ;
The little rills and waters numberlefs,

Inaudible by daylight, blend their notes
With the loud ſtreams : and often, at the hour
When iſſue forth the firſt pale ſtars, is heard,
Within the circuit of this fabric huge,
One voice—the ſolitary raven, flying
Athwart the concave of the dark blue dome,
Unſeen, perchance above the power of ſight—
An iron knell ! with echoes from afar
Faint—and ſtill fainter—as the cry, with which
The wanderer accompanies her flight
Through the calm region, fades upon the ear,
Diminiſhing by diſtance till it ſeemed
To expire ; yet from the abyſs is caught again,
And yet again recovered !

From " The Excurſion," Book IV.

THE IDLE SHEPHERD-BOYS; OR, DUNGEON-GHYLL FORCE.

A PASTORAL.

The valley rings with mirth and joy ;
Among the hills the echoes play
A never, never-ending ſong
To welcome in the May :

The magpie chatters with delight;
The mountain-raven's youngling brood
Have left the mother and the neft;
And they go rambling eaft and weft
In fearch of their own food;
Or through the glittering vapours dart
In very wantonnefs of heart.

Beneath a rock, upon the grafs,
Two boys are fitting in the fun;
It feems they have no work to do,
Or that their work is done.
On pipes of fycamore they play
The fragments of a Chriftmas hymn;
Or with that plant which in our dale
We call ftag-horn or fox's tail,
Their rufty hats they trim:
And thus, as happy as the day,
Thofe fhepherds wear the time away.

Along the river's ftony marge
The fand-lark chants a joyous fong;
The thrufh is bufy in the wood,
And carols loud and ftrong.
A thoufand lambs are on the rocks,
All newly-born! both earth and fky
Keep jubilee; and more than all,

G

Thofe boys with their green coronal ;
They never hear the cry,
That plaintive cry ! which up the hill
Comes from the depth of Dungeon-Ghyll.

Said Walter, leaping from the ground,
" Down to the ftump of yon old yew
We'll for our whiftles run a race."
——Away the fhepherds flew.
They leapt—they ran—and when they came
Right oppofite to Dungeon-Ghyll,
Seeing that he fhould lofe the prize,
" Stop ! " to his comrade Walter cries—
James ftopped with no good will :
Said Walter then, " Your tafk is here,
'Twill keep you working half a year.

" Now crofs where I fhall crofs—come on,
And follow me where I fhall lead."—
The other took him at his word,
But did not like the deed.
It was a fpot which you may fee
If ever you to Langdale go :
Into a chafm a mighty block
Hath fallen, and made a bridge of rock :
The gulf is deep below ;

And in a baſin black and ſmall
Receives a lofty waterfall.

With ſtaff in hand, acroſs the cleft
The challenger began his march ;
And now, all eyes and feet, hath gained
The middle of the arch.
When liſt ! he hears a piteous moan—
Again !—his heart within him dies—
His pulſe is ſtopped, his breath is loſt,
He totters, pale as any ghoſt,
And looking down, he ſpies
A lamb, that in the pool is pent
Within that black and frightful rent.

The lamb had ſlipped into the ſtream,
And ſafe, without a bruiſe or wound,
The cataract had borne him down
Into the gulf profound.
His dam had ſeen him when he fell,
She ſaw him down the torrent borne ;
And, while with all a mother's love
She from the lofty rocks above
Sent forth a cry forlorn,
The lamb, ſtill ſwimming round and round,
Made anſwer to that plaintive ſound.

When he had learnt what thing it was
That fent this rueful cry ; I ween,
The boy recovered heart, and told
The fight which he had feen.
Both gladly now deferred their tafk ;
Nor was there wanting other aid,—
A Poet, one who loves the brooks
Far better than the fages' books,
By chance had thither ftrayed ;
And there the helplefs lamb he found,
By thofe huge rocks encompaffed round.

He drew it gently from the pool,
And brought it forth into the light :
The fhepherds met him with his charge,
An unexpected fight !
Into their arms the lamb they took,
Said they, " He's neither maimed nor fcarred."
Then up the fteep afcent they hied,
And placed him at his mother's fide ;
And gently did the Bard
Thofe idle fhepherd-boys upbraid,
And bade them better mind their trade.

The Rotha.

TO JOANNA.

AMID the fmoke of cities did you pafs
    Your time of early youth ; and there you learned,
    From years of quiet induftry, to love
    The living beings by your own fire-fide,
    With fuch a ftrong devotion, that your heart
    Is flow towards the fympathies of them
    Who look upon the hills with tendernefs,
    And make dear friendfhips with the ftreams and
        groves.
Yet we, who are tranfgreffors in this kind,
Dwelling retired in our fimplicity
Among the woods and fields, we love you well,
Joanna ! and I guefs, fince you have been
So diftant from us now for two long years,
That you will gladly liften to difcourfe,

However trivial, if you thence are taught
That they, with whom you once were happy, talk
Familiarly of you and of old times.

While I was feated, now fome ten days paft,
Beneath thofe lofty firs that overtop
Their ancient neighbour, the old fteeple-tower,
The Vicar from his gloomy houfe hard by
Came forth to greet me; and when he had afked,
" How fares Joanna, that wild-hearted maid !
And when will fhe return to us ? " he paufed ;
And, after fhort exchange of village news,
He with grave looks demanded, for what caufe,
Reviving obfolete idolatry,
I, like a Runic prieft, in characters
Of formidable fize had chifelled out
Some uncouth name upon the native rock,
Above the Rotha, by the foreft fide.
—Now, by thofe dear immunities of heart
Engendered betwixt malice and true love,
I was not loth to be fo catechifed,
And this was my reply :—" As it befel,
One Summer morning we had walked abroad
At break of day, Joanna and myfelf.
—'Twas that delightful feafon when the broom,
Full-flowered, and vifible on every fteep,
Along the copfes runs in veins of gold.

Our pathway led us on to Rotha's banks ;
And when we came in front of that tall rock
Which looks towards the eaft, I there ftopped fhort,
And traced the lofty barrier with my eye
From bafe to fummit ; fuch delight I found
To note in fhrub and tree, in ftone and flower,
That intermixture of delicious hues,
Along fo vaft a furface, all at once,
In one impreffion, by connecting force
Of their own beauty, imaged in the heart.
—When I had gazed perhaps two minutes' fpace,
Joanna, looking in my eyes, beheld
That ravifhment of mine, and laughed aloud.
The rock, like fomething ftarting from a fleep,
Took up the lady's voice, and laughed again :
That ancient woman feated on Helm-Crag
Was ready with her cavern : Hammar-Scar,
And the tall fteep of Silver-How, fent forth
A noife of laughter ; fouthern Loughrigg heard,
And Fairfield anfwered with a mountain tone :
Helvellyn far into the clear blue fky
Carried the lady's voice—old Skiddaw blew
His fpeaking trumpet :—back out of the clouds
Of Glaramara fouthward came the voice ;
And Kirkftone toffed it from his mifty head.
—Now whether (faid I to our cordial friend,
Who in the hey-day of aftonifhment

Smiled in my face) this were in fimple truth
A work accomplifhed by the brotherhood
Of ancient mountains, or my ear was touched
With dreams and vifionary impulfes,
Is not for me to tell ; but fure I am
That there was a loud uproar in the hills :
And, while we both were liftening, to my fide
The fair Joanna drew, as if fhe wifhed
To fhelter from fome objeƈt of her fear.
—And hence, long afterwards, when eighteen moons
Were wafted, as I chanced to walk alone
Beneath this rock, at funrife, on a calm
And filent morning, I fat down, and there,
In memory of affeƈtions old and true,
I chifelled out in thofe rude charaƈters
Joanna's name upon the living ftone.
And I, and all who dwell by my fire-fide,
Have called the lovely rock, JOANNA's ROCK."

Rydale.

EMMA'S DELL.

I T was an April morning : frefh and clear,
The rivulet delighting in its ftrength,
Ran with a young man's fpeed ; and yet the voice
Of waters which the Winter had fupplied,
Was foftened down into a vernal tone.
The fpirit of enjoyment and defire,
And hopes and wifhes, from all living things
Went circling, like a multitude of founds.
The budding groves appeared as if in hafte
To fpur the fteps of June ; as if their fhades
Of various green were hindrances that ftood
Between them and their object : yet, meanwhile,
There was fuch deep contentment in the air,
That every naked afh, and tardy tree
Yet leaflefs, feemed as though the countenance

With which it looked on this delightful day
Were native to the Summer.—Up the brook
I roamed in the confuſion of my heart,
Alive to all things and forgetting all.
At length I to a ſudden turning came
In this continuous glen, where down a rock
The ſtream, ſo ardent in its courſe before,
Sent forth ſuch ſallies of glad ſound, that all
Which I till then had heard, appeared the voice
Of common pleaſure : beaſt and bird, the lamb,
The ſhepherd's dog, the linnet and the thruſh,
Vied with this waterfall, and made a ſong
Which, while I liſtened, ſeemed like the wild growth,
Or like ſome natural produce of the air,
That could not ceaſe to be.   Green leaves were here ;
But 'twas the foliage of the rocks, the birch,
The yew, the holly, and the bright green thorn,
With hanging iſlands of reſplendent furze :
And on a ſummit, diſtant a ſhort ſpace,
By any who ſhould look beyond the dell,
A ſingle mountain-cottage might be ſeen.
I gazed, and gazed, and to myſelf I ſaid,
" Our thoughts at leaſt are ours ; and this wild nook,
My EMMA, I will dedicate to thee."
———Soon did the ſpot become my other home,
My dwelling, and my out-of-doors abode.
And of the ſhepherds who have ſeen me there,

To whom I fometimes in our idle talk
Have told this fancy, two or three, perhaps,
Years after we are gone and in our graves,
When they have caufe to fpeak of this wild place,
May call it by the name of EMMA'S DELL.

WORDSWORTH'S HILL.

There is an eminence,—of thefe our hills
The laft that parleys with the fetting fun ;
We can behold it from our orchard-feat ;
And, when at evening we purfue our walk
Along the public way, this cliff, fo high
Above us, and fo diftant in its height,
Is vifible ; and often feems to fend
Its own deep quiet to reftore our hearts.
The meteors make of it a favourite haunt :
The ftar of Jove, fo beautiful and large
In the mid heavens, is never half fo fair
As when he fhines above it. 'Tis in truth
The lonelieft place we have among the clouds.
And fhe who dwells with me, whom I have loved
With fuch communion, that no place on earth
Can ever be a folitude to me,
Hath to this lonely fummit given my Name.

MARY WORDSWORTH'S NOOK.

TO M. H.

Our walk was far among the ancient trees ;
There was no road, nor any woodman's path ;
But the thick umbrage,—checking the wild growth
Of weed and fapling, on the foft green turf
Beneath the branches,—of itfelf had made
A track, which brought us to a flip of lawn,
And a fmall bed of water in the woods.
All round this pool both flocks and herds might drink
On its firm margin, even as from a well,
Or fome ftone bafin which the herdfman's hand
Had fhaped for their refrefhment ; nor did fun,
Or wind from any quarter, ever come,
But as a bleffing, to this calm recefs,
This glade of water, and this one green field.
The fpot was made by Nature for herfelf.
The travellers know it not, and 'twill remain
Unknown to them : but it is beautiful ;
And if a man fhould plant his cottage near,
Should fleep beneath the fhelter of its trees,
And blend its waters with his daily meal,

He would fo love it, that in his death-hour
Its image would furvive among his thoughts :
And therefore, my fweet MARY, this ftill nook,
With all its beeches, we have named from you.

WRITTEN WITH A SLATE-PENCIL

Upon a Stone, the largeft of a Heap lying near a Deferted Quarry,
upon one of the Iflands at Rydale.

Stranger ! this hillock of misfhapen ftones
Is not a Ruin of the ancient time,
Nor, as perchance thou rafhly deem'ft, the Cairn
Of fome old Britifh chief : 'tis nothing more
Than the rude embryo of a little dome
Or pleafure-houfe, once deftined to be built
Among the birch-trees of this rocky ifle.
But, as it chanced, Sir William having learned
That from the fhore a full-grown man might wade,
And make himfelf a freeman of this fpot
At any hour he chofe, the knight forthwith
Defifted, and the quarry and the mound
Are monuments of his unfinifhed tafk.——

The block on which thefe lines are traced, perhaps,
Was once felected as the corner-ftone
Of the intended pile, which would have been
Some quaint odd play-thing of elaborate fkill,
So that, I guefs, the linnet and the thrufh,
And other little builders who dwell here,
Had wondered at the work. But blame him not,
For old Sir William was a gentle knight
Bred in this vale, to which he appertained
With all his anceftry. Then peace to him,
And for the outrage which he had devifed
Entire forgivenefs!——But if thou art one
On fire with thy impatience to become
An inmate of thefe mountains,—if, difturbed
By beautiful conceptions, thou haft hewn
Out of the quiet rock the elements
Of thy trim manfion deftined foon to blaze
In fnow-white fplendour,—think again, and, taught
By old Sir William and his quarry, leave
Thy fragments to the bramble and the rofe;
There let the vernal flow-worm fun himfelf,
And let the red-breaft hop from ftone to ftone.

TO MY SISTER.

*Written at a small distance from my House,
and sent by my little Boy.*

It is the first mild day of March :
Each minute sweeter than before,
The red-breast sings from the tall larch
That stands beside our door.

There is a blessing in the air,
Which seems a sense of joy to yield
To the bare trees, and mountains bare,
And grass in the green field.

My Sister ! ('tis a wish of mine)
Now that our morning meal is done,
Make haste, your morning task resign ;
Come forth and feel the sun.

Edward will come with you ; and pray,
Put on with fpeed your woodland drefs ;
And bring no book : for this one day
We'll give to idlenefs.

No joylefs forms fhall regulate
Our living calendar :
We from to-day, my friend, will date
The opening of the year.

Love, now an univerfal birth,
From heart to heart is ftealing,
From earth to man, from man to earth :
—It is the hour of feeling.

One moment now may give us more
Than fifty years of reafon :
Our minds fhall drink at every pore
The fpirit of the feafon.

Some filent laws our hearts may make,
Which they fhall long obey :
We for the year to come may take
Our temper from to-day.

And from the bleſſed power that rolls
About, below, above,
We'll frame the meaſure of our ſouls :
They ſhall be tuned to love.

Then come, my Siſter ! come, I pray,
With ſpeed put on your woodland dreſs ;
And bring no book : for this one day
We'll give to idleneſs.

Grafmere.

❧❦❧

FLY, fome kind fpirit, fly to Grafmere Vale!
Say that we come, and come by this day's light:
Glad tidings!—fpread them over field and height;
But chiefly let one cottage hear the tale;
There let a myftery of joy prevail,
The kitten frolic with unruly might,
And Rover whine, as at a fecond fight
Of near-approaching good that fhall not fail;—
And from that infant's face let joy appear;
Yea, let our Mary's one companion child,
That hath her fix wecks' folitude beguiled
With intimations manifold and dear,
While we have wandered over wood and wild,
Smile on his Mother now with bolder cheer.

A WALK BY THE LAKE.

A narrow girdle of rough ftones and crags,
A rude and natural caufeway interpofed
Between the water and a winding flope
Of copfe and thicket, leaves the eaftern fhore
Of Grafmere fafe in its own privacy.
And there, myfelf and two beloved Friends,
One calm September morning, ere the mift
Had altogether yielded to the fun,
Sauntered on this retired and difficult way.
——Ill fuits the road with one in hafte, but we
Played with our time ; and, as we ftrolled along,
It was our occupation to obferve
Such objects as the waves had toffed afhore,
Feather, or leaf, or weed, or withered bough,
Each on the other heaped, along the line
Of the dry wreck.   And, in our vacant mood,
Not feldom did we ftop to watch fome tuft
Of dandelion feed or thiftle's beard,
That fkimmed the furface of the dead calm lake,
Suddenly halting now—a lifelefs ftand !
And ftarting off again with freak as fudden ;
In all its fportive wanderings, all the while,
Making report of an invifible breeze,

That was its wings, its chariot, and its horfe,
Its very playmate, and its moving foul.
——And often, trifling with a privilege
Alike indulged to all, we paufed, one now,
And now the other, to point out, perchance
To pluck, fome flower or water-weed, too fair
Either to be divided from the place
On which it grew, or to be left alone
To its own beauty.   Many fuch there are,
Fair ferns and flowers, and chiefly that tall fern
So ftately, of the Queen Ofmunda named,
Plant lovelier in its own retired abode
On Grafmere's beach, than Naiad by the fide
Of Grecian brook, or Lady of the Mere,
Sole-fitting by the fhores of old Romance.
—So fared we that fweet morning : from the fields
Meanwhile a noife was heard, the bufy mirth
Of reapers, men and women, boys and girls.
Delighted much to liften to thofe founds,
And, in the fafhion which I have defcribed,
Feeding unthinking fancies, we advanced
Along the indented fhore ; when fuddenly,
Through a thin veil of glittering haze, we faw
Before us, on a point of jutting land,
The tall and upright figure of a man
Attired in peafant's garb, who ftood alone,
Angling befide the margin of the lake.

That way we turned our fteps ; nor was it long
Ere, making ready comments on the fight
Which then we faw, with one and the fame voice
Did all cry out, that he muft be indeed
An idler, he who thus could lofe a day
Of the mid-harveft, when the labourer's hire
Is ample, and fome little might be ftored
Wherewith to cheer him in the winter-time.
Thus talking of that peafant, we approached
Clofe to the fpot where with his rod and line
He ftood alone ; whereat he turned his head
To greet us—and we faw a man worn down
By ficknefs, gaunt and lean, with funken cheeks
And wafted limbs, his legs fo long and lean,
That for my fingle felf I looked at them,
Forgetful of the body they fuftained.—
Too weak to labour in the harveft field,
The man was ufing his beft fkill to gain
A pittance from the dead unfeeling lake
That knew not of his wants. I will not fay
What thoughts immediately were ours, nor how
The happy idlenefs of that fweet morn,
With all its lovely images, was changed
To ferious mufing and to felf-reproach.
Nor did we fail to fee within ourfelves
What need there is to be referved in fpeech,
And temper all our thoughts with charity.

—Therefore, unwilling to forget that day,
My friend, myfelf, and fhe who then received
The fame admonifhment, have called the place
By a memorial name, uncouth indeed
As e'er by mariner was given to bay
Or foreland, on a new-difcovered coaft ;
And POINT RASH JUDGMENT is the name it bears.

HELM CRAG.

The road is black before his eyes,
Glimmering faintly where it lies;
Black is the fky—and every hill,
Up to the fky, is blacker ftill—
Sky, hill, and dale, one difmal room,
Hung round and overhung with gloom ;
Save that above a fingle height
Is to be feen a lurid light,
Above Helm Crag—a ftreak half dead,
A burning of portentous red ;
And near that lurid light, full well
The Aftrologer, fage Sidrophel,
Where at his defk and book he fits,
Puzzling aloft his curious wits;
He whofe domain is held in common
With no one but the ANCIENT WOMAN,

Cowering befide her rifted cell,
As if intent on magic fpell ;—
Dread pair, that fpite of wind and weather,
Still fit upon Helm Crag together !

From " The Waggoner," Canto I.

WRITTEN WITH A PENCIL

Upon a Stone in the Wall of the Houfe (an Out-Houfe) on the Ifland at Grafmere.

Rude is this edifice, and thou haft feen
Buildings, albeit rude, that have maintained
Proportions more harmonious, and approached
To fomewhat of a clofer fellowfhip
With the ideal grace.   Yet, as it is,
Do take it in good part :—alas, the poor
Vitruvius of our village had no help
From the great city ; never, on the leaves
Of red morocco folio, faw difplayed
The fkeletons and pre-exifting ghosts
Of beauties yet unborn,—the ruftic box,
Snug cot, with coach-houfe, fhed, and hermitage.
Thou feeft a homely pile, yet to thefe walls
The heifer comes in the fnow-ftorm, and here

The new-dropped lamb finds fhelter from the wind.
And hither does one Poet fometimes row
His pinnace, a fmall vagrant barge, up-piled
With plenteous ftore of heath and withered fern
(A lading which he with his fickle cuts
Among the mountains), and beneath this roof
He makes his Summer couch, and here at noon
Spreads out his limbs, while, yet unfhorn, the fheep,
Panting beneath the burden of their wool,
Lie round him, even as if they were a part
Of his own houfehold; nor, while from his bed,
He through that door-place looks towards the lake
And to the ftirring breezes, does he want
Creations lovely as the work of fleep,
Fair fights and vifions of romantic joy!

MICHAEL.

A PASTORAL POEM.

If from the public way you turn your fteps
Up the tumultuous brook of Greenhead Ghyll,
You will fuppofe that with an upright path
Your feet muft ftruggle ; in fuch bold afcent
The paftoral mountains front you, face to face.
But, courage ! for around that boifterous brook

The mountains have all opened out themfelves,
And made a hidden valley of their own.
No habitation there is feen ; but fuch
As journey thither find themfelves alone
With a few fheep, with rocks and ftones, and kites
That overhead are failing in the fky.
It is, in truth, an utter folitude ;
Nor fhould I have made mention of this dell,
But for one objeɕ which you might pafs by,
Might fee and notice not.   Befide the brook
There is a ftraggling heap of unhewn ftones ;
And to that place a ftory appertains,
Which, though it be ungarnifhed with events,
Is not unfit, I deem, for the fire-fide,
Or for the Summer fhade.   It was the firft,
The earlieft of thofe tales that fpake to me
Of fhepherds, dwellers in the valleys, men
Whom I already loved ;—not verily
For their own fakes, but for the fields and hills
Where was their occupation and abode.
And hence this tale,—while I was yet a boy
Carelefs of books, yet having felt the power
Of Nature,—by the gentle agency
Of natural objeɕs, led me on to feel
For paffions that were not my own, and think
(At random, and imperfeɕly indeed)
On man, the heart of man, and human life.

Therefore, although it be a hiftory
Homely and rude, I will relate the fame
For the delight of a few natural hearts ;
And, with yet fonder feeling, for the fake
Of youthful poets, who among thefe hills
Will be my fecond felf when I am gone.

Upon the foreft-fide in Grafmere Vale
There dwelt a fhepherd, Michael was his name ;
An old man, ftout of heart, and ftrong of limb.
His bodily frame had been from youth to age
Of an unufual ftrength : his mind was keen,
Intenfe and frugal, apt for all affairs,
And in his fhepherd's calling he was prompt
And watchful more than ordinary men.
Hence he had learned the meaning of all winds,
Of blafts of every tone ; and, oftentimes,
When others heeded not, he heard the fouth
Make fubterraneous mufic, like the noife
Of bagpipers on diftant Highland hills.
The fhepherd, at fuch warning, of his flock
Bethought him, and he to himfelf would fay,
" The winds are now devifing work for me ! "
And, truly, at all times, the ftorm, that drives
The traveller to a fhelter, fummoned him
Up to the mountains : he had been alone
Amid the heart of many thoufand mifts,

That came to him and left him on the heights.
So lived he till his eightieth year was paſt;
And groſſly that man errs, who ſhould ſuppoſe
That the green valleys, and the ſtreams and rocks,
Were things indifferent to the ſhepherd's thoughts.
Fields, where with cheerful ſpirits he had breathed
The common air; the hills, which he ſo oft
Had climbed with vigorous ſteps; which had impreſſed
So many incidents upon his mind
Of hardſhip, ſkill, or courage, joy or fear;
Which, like a book, preſerved the memory
Of the dumb animals whom he had ſaved,
Had fed or ſheltered, linking to ſuch acts,
So grateful in themſelves, the certainty
Of honourable gain; theſe fields, theſe hills,
Which were his living being, even more
Than his own blood—what could they leſs? had laid
Strong hold on his affections, were to him
A pleaſurable feeling of blind love,
The pleaſure which there is in life itſelf.

His days had not been paſſed in ſingleneſs.
His helpmate was a comely matron, old—
Though younger than himſelf full twenty years.
She was a woman of a ſtirring life,
Whoſe heart was in her houſe : two wheels ſhe had
Of antique form ; this large, for ſpinning wool ;

That fmall, for flax ; and if one wheel had reft,
It was becaufe the other was at work.
The pair had but one inmate in their houfe,
An only child, who had been born to them
When Michael, telling o'er his years, began
To deem that he was old,—in fhepherd's phrafe,
With one foot in the grave. This only fon,
With two brave fheep-dogs tried in many a ftorm,
The one of an ineftimable worth,
Made all their houfehold. I may truly fay,
That they were as a proverb in the vale
For endlefs induftry. When day was gone,
And from their occupations out of doors
The fon and father were come home, even then
Their labour did not ceafe ; unlefs when all
Turned to the cleanly fupper-board, and there,
Each with a mefs of pottage and fkimmed milk,
Sat round their bafket piled with oaten cakes,
And their plain home-made cheefe. Yet when their
        meal
Was ended, Luke (for fo the fon was named)
And his old father both betook themfelves
To fuch convenient work as might employ
Their hands by the fire-fide ; perhaps to card
Wool for the houfewife's fpindle, or repair
Some injury done to fickle, flail, or fcythe,
Or other implement of houfe or field.

Down from the ceiling, by the chimney's edge,
Which in our ancient uncouth country ftyle
Did with a huge projection overbrow
Large fpace beneath, as duly as the light
Of day grew dim, the houfewife hung a lamp ;
An aged utenfil, which had performed
Service beyond all others of its kind.
Early at evening did it burn, and late,
Surviving comrade of uncounted hours,
Which going by from year to year had found
And left the couple neither gay perhaps
Nor cheerful, yet with objects and with hopes,
Living a life of eager induftry.
And now, when Luke was in his eighteenth year,
There by the light of this old lamp they fat,
Father and fon, while late into the night
The houfewife plied her own peculiar work,
Making the cottage through the filent hours
Murmur as with the found of fummer flies.
This light was famous in its neighbourhood,
And was a public fymbol of the life
The thrifty pair had lived.   For, as it chanced,
Their cottage on a plot of rifing ground
Stood fingle, with large profpect, north and fouth,
High into Eafedale, up to Dunmail-Raife,
And weftward to the village near the lake ;
And from this conftant light, fo regular

And fo far feen, the houfe itfelf, by all
Who dwelt within the limits of the vale,
Both old and young, was named the EVENING STAR.

Thus living on through fuch a length of years,
The fhepherd, if he loved himfelf, muft needs
Have loved his helpmate ; but to Michael's heart
This fon of his old age was yet more dear—
Effect which might perhaps have been produced
By that inftinctive tendernefs, the fame
Blind fpirit, which is in the blood of all—
Or that a child, more than all other gifts,
Brings hope with it, and forward-looking thoughts,
And ftirrings of inquietude, when they
By tendency of nature needs muft fail.

From fuch and other caufes, to the thoughts
Of the old man his only fon was now
The deareft object that he knew on earth.
Exceeding was the love he bare to him,
His heart and his heart's joy ! For oftentimes
Old Michael, while he was a babe in arms,
Had done him female fervice, not alone
For dalliance and delight, as is the ufe
Of fathers, but with patient mind enforced
To acts of tendernefs ; and he had rocked
His cradle with a woman's gentle hand.

And, in a later time, ere yet the boy
Had put on boy's attire, did Michael love,
Albeit of a ſtern unbending mind,
To have the young one in his ſight, when he
Had work by his own door, or when he ſat,
With ſheep before him, on his ſhepherd's ſtool,
Beneath that large old oak, which near their door
Stood,—and, from its enormous breadth of ſhade,
Choſen for the ſhearer's covert from the ſun,
Thence in our ruſtic dialect was called
The CLIPPING TREE, a name which yet it bears.

There, while they two were ſitting in the ſhade,
With others round them, earneſt all and blithe,
Would Michael exerciſe his heart with looks
Of fond correction and reproof beſtowed
Upon the child, if he diſturbed the ſheep
By catching at their legs, or with his ſhouts
Scared them, while they lay ſtill beneath the ſhears.

And when by Heaven's good grace the boy grew up
A healthy lad, and carried in his cheek
Two ſteady roſes that were five years old,
Then Michael from a winter coppice cut
With his own hand a ſapling, which he hooped
With iron, making it throughout in all
Due requiſites a perfect ſhepherd's ſtaff,

And gave it to the boy ; wherewith equipt
He as a watchman oftentimes was placed
At gate or gap, to ftem or turn the flock ;
And, to his office prematurely called,
There ftood the urchin, as you will divine,
Something between a hindrance and a help ;
And for this caufe, not always, I believe,
Receiving from his father hire of praife ;
Though ncught was left undone which ftaff, or voice,
Or looks, or threatening geftures, could perform.

But foon as Luke, full ten years old, could ftand
Against the mountain blafts ; and to the heights,
Not fearing toil, nor length of weary ways,
He with his father daily went, and they
Were as companions, why fhould I relate
That objeέts which the fhepherd loved before
Were dearer now ? that from the boy there came
Feelings and emanations—things which were
Light to the fun and mufic to the wind ;
And that the old man's heart feemed born again ?

Thus in his father's fight the boy grew up ;
And now, when he had reached his eighteenth year,
He was his comfort and his daily hope.

While in this fort the fimple houfehold lived
From day to day, to Michael's ear there came

Diftrefsful tidings. Long before the time
Of which I fpeak, the fhepherd had been bound
In furety for his brother's fon, a man
Of an induftrious life, and ample means,—
But unforefeen misfortunes fuddenly
Had preffed upon him,—and old Michael now
Was fummoned to difcharge the forfeiture,
A grievous penalty, but little lefs
Than half his fubftance. This unlooked-for claim,
At the firft hearing, for a moment took
More hope out of his life than he fuppofed
That any old man ever could have loft.
As foon as he had gathered fo much ftrength
That he could look his trouble in the face,
It feemed that his fole refuge was to fell
A portion of his patrimonial fields.
Such was his firft refolve ; he thought again,
And his heart failed him. "Ifabel," faid he,
Two evenings after he had heard the news,
"I have been toiling more than feventy years,
And in the open funfhine of God's love
Have we all lived ; yet if thefe fields of ours
Should pafs into a ftranger's hand, I think
That I could not lie quiet in my grave.
Our lot is a hard lot ; the fun himfelf
Has fcarcely been more diligent than I,
And I have lived to be a fool at laft

To my own family. An evil man
That was, and made an evil choice, if he
Were falfe to us ; and, if he were not falfe,
There are ten thoufand to whom lofs like this
Had been no forrow. I forgive him ;—but
'Twere better to be dumb than to talk thus.

    " When I began, my purpofe was to fpeak
Of remedies and of a cheerful hope.
Our Luke fhall leave us, Ifabel ; the land
Shall not go from us, and it fhall be free ;
He fhall poffefs it, free as is the wind
That paffes over it. We have, thou know'ft,
Another kinfman—he will be our friend
In this diftress. He is a profperous man,
Thriving in trade—and Luke to him fhall go,
And with his kinfman's help and his own thrift,
He quickly will repair this lofs, and then
May come again to us. If here he ftay,
What can be done ? Where every one is poor
What can be gained ? " At this the old man paufed,
And Ifabel fat filent, for her mind
Was bufy, looking back into paft times.
There's Richard Bateman, thought fhe to herfelf,
He was a parifh-boy—at the church-door
They made a gathering for him, fhillings, pence,
And half-pennies, wherewith the neighbours bought

A balket, which they filled with pedlar's wares ;
And, with this balket on his arm, the lad
Went up to London, found a malter there,
Who out of many chofe the trufty boy
To go and overlook his merchandize
Beyond the feas ; where he grew wondrous rich,
And left eftates and moneys to the poor,
And at his birth-place built a chapel floored
With marble, which he fent from foreign lands.
Thefe thoughts, and many others of like fort,
Paffed quickly through the mind of Ifabel,
And her face brightened.   The old man was glad,
And thus refumed :—" Well, Ifabel ! this fcheme
Thefe two days has been meat and drink to me.
Far more than we have loft is left us yet.
—We have enough—I wifh, indeed, that I
Were younger ;—but this hope is a good hope.
—Make ready Luke's beft garments, of the beft
Buy for him more, and let us fend him forth
To-morrow, or the next day, or to-night :
—If he could go, the boy fhould go to-night."

    Here Michael ceafed, and to the fields went forth
With a light heart.   The houfewife for five days
Was reftlefs morn and night, and all day long
Wrought on with her beft fingers to prepare
Things needful for the journey of her fon.

But Ifabel was glad when Sunday came
To ftop her in her work : for, when fhe lay
By Michael's fide, fhe through the two laft nights
Heard him, how he was troubled in his fleep :
And when they rofe at morning fhe could fee
That all his hopes were gone.   That day at noon
She faid to Luke, while they two by themfelves
Were fitting at the door, " Thou muft not go :
We have no other child but thee to lofe,
None to remember—do not go away,
For if thou leave thy father he will die."
The youth made anfwer with a jocund voice ;
And Ifabel, when fhe had told her fears,
Recovered heart.   That evening her beft fare
Did fhe bring forth, and all together fat
Like happy people round a Chriftmas fire.

    Next morning Ifabel refumed her work ;
And all the enfuing week the houfe appeared
As cheerful as a grove in Spring : at length
The expected letter from their kinfman came,
With kind affurances that he would do
His utmoft for the welfare of the boy ;
To which requefts were added that forthwith
He might be fent to him.   Ten times or more
The letter was read over ; Ifabel
Went forth to fhow it to the neighbours round ;

Nor was there at that time on Englifh land
A prouder heart than Luke's.   When Ifabel
Had to her houfe returned, the old man faid,
" He fhall depart to-morrow."   To this word
The houfewife anfwered, talking much of things
Which, if at fuch fhort notice he fhould go,
Would furely be forgotten.   But at length
She gave confent, and Michael was at eafe.

    Near the tumultuous brook of Greenhead Ghyll,
In that deep valley, Michael had defigned
To build a fheepfold ; and, before he heard
The tidings of his melancholy lofs,
For this fame purpofe he had gathered up
A heap of ftones, which by the ftreamlet's edge
Lay thrown together, ready for the work.
With Luke that evening thitherward he walked ;
And foon as they had reached the place, he ftopped,
And thus the old man fpake to him :—" My fon,
To-morrow thou wilt leave me : with full heart
I look upon thee, for thou art the fame
That wert a promife to me ere thy birth,
And all thy life haft been my da'ly joy.
I will relate to thee fome little part
Of our two hiftories ; 't will do thee good
When thou art from me, even if I fhould fpeak
Of things thou canft not know of.——After thou

Firſt cam'ſt into the world—as oft befals
To new-born infants—thou didſt ſleep away
Two days, and bleſſings from thy father's tongue
Then fell upon thee.   Day by day paſſed on,
And ſtill I loved thee with increaſing love.
Never to living ear came ſweeter ſounds
Than when I heard thee by our own fireſide
Firſt uttering, without words, a natural tune ;
When thou, a feeding babe, didſt in thy joy
Sing at thy mother's breaſt.   Month followed month,
And in the open fields my life was paſſed,
And on the mountains, elſe I think that thou
Hadſt been brought up upon thy father's knees.
But we were playmates, Luke : among theſe hills,
As well thou know'ſt, in us the old and young
Have played together, nor with me didſt thou
Lack any pleaſure which a boy can know."
Luke had a manly heart : but at theſe words
He ſobbed aloud.   The old man graſped his hand,
And ſaid, " Nay, do not take it ſo—I ſee
That theſe are things of which I need not ſpeak.
—Even to the utmoſt I have been to thee
A kind and a good father : and herein
I but repay a gift which I myſelf
Received at other's hands ; for, though now old
Beyond the common life of man, I ſtill
Remember them who loved me in my youth.

Both of them fleep together: here they lived,
As all their forefathers had done ; and when
At length their time was come, they were not loth
To give their bodies to the family mould.
I wifhed that thou fhouldft live the life they lived.
But 'tis a long time to look back, my fon,
And fee fo little gain from fixty years.
Thefe fields were burthened when they came to me ;
Till I was forty years of age, not more
Than half of my inheritance was mine.
I toiled and toiled ; God bleffed me in my work,
And till thefe three weeks paft the land was free.
—It looks as if it never could endure
Another mafter.   Heaven forgive me, Luke,
If I judge ill for thee, but it feems good
That thou fhouldft go."

                              At this the old man paufed;
Then pointing to the ftones near which they ftood,
Thus, after a fhort filence, he refumed :
" This was a work for us ; and now, my fon,
It is a work for me.   But, lay one ftone—
Here, lay it for me, Luke, with thine own hands.
Nay, boy, be of good hope ;—we both may live
To fee a better day.   At eighty-four
I ftill am ftrong and ftout ;—do thou thy part,
I will do mine.—I will begin again

With many tafks that were refigned to thee ;
Up to the heights, and in among the ftorms,
Will I without thee go again, and do
All works which I was wont to do alone,
Before I knew thy face.—Heaven blefs thee, boy !
Thy heart thefe two weeks has been beating faft
With many hopes ; it fhould be fo—yes—yes—
I knew that thou couldft never have a wifh
To leave me, Luke : thou haft been bound to me
Only by links of love : when thou art gone,
What will be left to us !—But, I forget
My purpofes. Lay now the corner-ftone,
As I requefted ; and hereafter, Luke,
When thou art gone away, fhould evil men
Be thy companions, think of me, my fon,
And of this moment ; hither turn thy thoughts,
And God will ftrengthen thee : amid all fear
And all temptation, Luke, I pray that thou
Mayft bear in mind the life thy fathers lived,
Who, being innocent, did for that caufe
Beftir them in good deeds. Now, fare thee well—
When thou return'ft, thou in this place wilt fee
A work which is not here : a covenant
'I' will be between us——But, whatever fate
Befal thee, I fhall love thee to the laft,
And bear thy memory with me to the grave."

The fhepherd ended here : and Luke ftooped down,
And as his father had requefted, laid
The firft ftone of the fheepfold.   At the fight
The old man's grief broke from him, to his heart
He preffed his fon, he kiffèd him and wept :
And to the houfe together they returned.
—Hufhed was that houfe in peace, or feeming peace,
Ere the night fell :—with morrow's dawn the boy
Began his journey, and when he had reached
The public way, he put on a bold face ;
And all the neighbours, as he paffed their doors,
Came forth with wifhes and with farewell prayers,
That followed him till he was out of fight.

A good report did from their kinfman come,
Of Luke and his well-doing : and the boy
Wrote loving letters, full of wondrous news,
Which, as the houfewife phrafed it, were throughout
" The prettieft letters that were ever feen."
Both parents read them with rejoicing hearts.
So, many months paffed on : and once again
The fhepherd went about his daily work
With confident and cheerful thoughts ; and now
Sometimes when he could find a leifure hour,
He to that valley took his way, and there
Wrought at the fheepfold.   Meantime Luke began
To flacken in his duty ; and at length

M

He in the diſſolute city gave himſelf
To evil courſes : ignominy and ſhame
Fell on him, ſo that he was driven at laſt
To ſeek a hiding-place beyond the ſeas.

  There is a comfort in the ſtrength of love ;
'Twill make a thing endurable, which elſe
Would break the heart :—old Michael found it ſo.
I have converſed with more than one who well
Remembered the old man, and what he was
Years after he had heard this heavy news.
His bodily frame had been from youth to age
Of an unuſual ſtrength.   Among the rocks
He went, and ſtill looked up upon the ſun,
And liſtened to the wind ; and as before
Performed all kinds of labour for his ſheep,
And for the land, his ſmall inheritance.
And to that hollow dell from time to time
Did he repair, to build the fold of which
His flock had need.   'Tis not forgotten yet,
The pity which was then in every heart
For the old man—and 'tis believed by all
That many and many a day he thither went,
And never lifted up a ſingle ſtone.

  There, by the ſheepfold, ſometimes was he ſeen
Sitting alone, or with his faithful dog,

Then old, befide him, lying at his feet.
The length of full feven years, from time to time,
He at the building of this fheepfold wrought,
And left the work unfinifhed when he died.
Three years, or little more, did Ifabel
Survive her hufband : at her death the eftate
Was fold, and went into a ftranger's hand.
The cottage which was named the EVENING STAR
Is gone—the ploughfhare has been through the ground
On which it ftood ; great changes have been wrought
In all the neighbourhood :—yet the oak is left
That grew befide their door ; and the remains
Of the unfinifhed fheepfold may be feen
Befide the boifterous brook of Greenhead Ghyll.

A FAREWELL.

(Written when going to bring home his Bride.)

Farewell, thou little nook of mountain-ground,
Thou rocky corner in the loweft ftair
Of that magnificent temple which doth bound
One fide of our whole vale with grandeur rare ;
Sweet garden-orchard, eminently fair,

The lovelieſt ſpot that man hath ever found,
Farewell!—We leave thee to Heaven's peaceful care,
Thee, and the cottage which thou doſt ſurround.

Our boat is ſafely anchored by the ſhore,
And ſafely ſhe will ride when we are gone ;
The flowering ſhrubs that decorate our door
Will proſper, though untended and alone :
Fields, goods, and far-off chattels we have none ;
Theſe narrow bounds contain our private ſtore
Of things earth makes, and ſun doth ſhine upon ;
Here are they in our ſight—we have no more.

Sunſhine and ſhower be with you, bud and bell !
For two months now in vain we ſhall be ſought :
We leave you here in ſolitude to dwell
With theſe our lateſt gifts of tender thought ;
Thou, like the morning, in thy ſaffron coat,
Bright gowan, and marſh-marigold, farewell !
Whom from the borders of the lake we brought,
And placed together near our rocky well.

We go for one to whom you will be dear ;
And ſhe will prize this bower, this Indian ſhed,
Our own contrivance, building without peer !
—A gentle maid, whoſe heart is lowly bred,
Whoſe pleaſures are in wild fields gatherèd,

With joyoufnefs, and with a thoughtful cheer,
She 'll come to you,—to you herfelf will wed,—
And love the bleffed life which we lead here.

Dear fpot ! which we have watched with tender heed,
Bringing thee chofen plants and bloffoms blown
Among the diftant mountains, flower and weed,
Which thou haft taken to thee as thy own,
Making all kindnefs regiftered and known ;
Thou for our fakes, though Nature's child indeed,
Fair in thyfelf and beautiful alone,
Haft taken gifts which thou doft little need.

And O moft conftant, yet moft fickle place,
Thou haft thy wayward moods, as thou doft fhow
To them who look not daily on thy face ;
Who, being loved, in love no bounds doft know,
And fay'ft when we forfake thee, " Let them go ! "
Thou eafy-hearted thing, with thy wild race
Of weeds and flowers, till we return be flow,—
And travel with the year at a foft pace.

Help us to tell her tales of years gone by,
And this fweet fpring, the beft beloved and beft ;
Joy will be flown in its mortality ;
Something muft ftay to tell us of the reft.
Here, thronged with primrofes, the fteep rock's breaft

Glittered at evening like a ſtarry ſky ;
And in this buſh our ſparrow built her neſt,
Of which I ſang one ſong that will not die.

O happy Garden ! whoſe ſecluſion deep
Hath been ſo friendly to induſtrious hours ;
And to ſoft ſlumbers, that did gently ſteep
Our ſpirits, carrying with them dreams of flowers,
And wild notes warbled among leafy bowers !
Two burning months let Summer overleap,
And, coming back with her who will be ours,
Into thy boſom we again ſhall creep.

Helvellyn.

FIDELITY.

A BARKING found the fhepherd hears,
A cry as of a dog or fox ;
He halts, and fearches with his eyes
Among the fcattered rocks :
And now at diftance can difcern
A ftirring in a brake of fern ;
And inftantly a dog is feen,
Glancing from that covert green.

The dog is not of mountain breed ;
Its motions, too, are wild and fhy ;
With fomething, as the fhepherd thinks,
Unufual in its cry :

Nor is there any one in fight
All round, in hollow or on height ;
Nor fhout, nor whiftle ftrikes his ear ;
What is the creature doing here ?

It was a cove, a huge recefs,
That keeps, till June, December's fnow ;
A lofty precipice in front,
A filent tarn below !
Far in the bofom of Helvellyn,
Remote from public road or dwelling,
Pathway, or cultivated land ;
From trace of human foot or hand.

There fometimes doth a leaping fifh
Send through the tarn a lonely cheer ;
The crags repeat the raven's croak,
In fymphony auftere ;
Thither the rainbow comes—the cloud—
And mifts that fpread the flying fhroud ;
And funbeams ; and the founding blaft,
That, if it could, would hurry paft,
But that enormous barrier binds it faft.

Not free from boding thoughts, a while
The fhepherd ftood : then makes his way

Towards the dog, o'er rocks and ftones,
As quickly as he may ;
Nor far had gone, before he found
A human fkeleton on the ground ;
The appalled difcoverer, with a figh
Looks round, to learn the hiftory.

From thofe abrupt and perilous rocks
The man had fallen, that place of fear !
At length upon the fhepherd's mind
It breaks, and all is clear :
He inftantly recalled the name,
And who he was, and whence he came ;
Remembered, too, the very day
On which the traveller paffed this way.

But hear a wonder, for whofe fake,
This lamentable tale I tell !
A lafting monument of words
This wonder merits well.
The dog, which ftill was hovering nigh,
Repeating the fame timid cry,
This dog had been through three months' fpace
A dweller in that favage place.

Yes, proof was plain that fince the day
On which the traveller thus had died,

N

The dog had watched about the fpot,
Or by his mafter's fide ;
How nourifhed here through fuch long time
He knows, who gave that love fublime,
And gave that ftrength of feeling, great
Above all human eftimate.

"'TIS SAID THAT SOME HAVE DIED FOR LOVE."

'Tis faid that fome have died for love :
And here and there a churchyard grave is found
In the cold North's unhallowed ground,—
Becaufe the wretched man himfelf had flain,
His love was fuch a grievous pain.
And there is one whom I five years have known ;
He dwells alone
Upon Helvellyn's fide :
He loved.—The pretty Barbara died,
And thus he made his moan :
Three years had Barbara in her grave been laid,
When thus his moan he made :—

　　" Oh, move, thou cottage, from behind that oak !
Or let the aged tree uprooted lie,

That in fome other way yon fmoke
May mount into the fky !
The clouds pafs on ; they from the heavens depart.
I look—the fky is empty fpace ;
I know not what I trace ;
But, when I ceafe to look, my hand is on my heart.

" O, what a weight is in thefe fhades ! ye leaves,
When will that dying murmur be fuppreff'd ?
Your found my heart of peace bereaves,
It robs my heart of reft.
Thou thrufh, that fingeft loud—and loud and free,
Into yon row of willows flit,
Upon that alder fit,
Or fing another fong, or choofe another tree.

" Roll back, fweet rill ! back to thy mountain bounds,
And there for ever be thy waters chain'd !
For thou doft haunt the air with founds
That cannot be fuftain'd ;
If ftill beneath that pine-tree's ragged bough
Headlong yon waterfall muft come,
Oh let it then be dumb !—
Be anything, fweet rill, but that which thou art now.

" Thou eglantine, whofe arch fo proudly towers
(Even like a rainbow fpanning half the vale),

Thou one fair fhrub—oh, fhed thy flowers,
And ftir not in the gale !
For thus to fee thee nodding in the air,—
To fee thy arch thus ftretch and bend,
Thus rife and thus defcend,—
Difturbs me, till the fight is more than I can bear."

The man who makes this feverifh complaint
Is one of giant ftature, who could dance
Equipp'd from head to foot in iron mail.
Ah gentle love ! if ever thought was thine
To ftore up kindred hours for me, thy face
Turn from me, gentle love ! nor let me walk
Within the found of Emma's voice, or know
Such happinefs as I have known to-day.

Derwent-water.

SONNET TO SKIDDAW.

ELION and Offa flourifh fide by fide,
Together in immortal books enrolled :
His ancient dower Olympus hath not fold ;
And that infpiring hill, which " did divide
Into two ample horns his forehead wide,"
Shines with poetic radiance as of old ;
While not an Englifh mountain we behold
By the celeftial mufes glorified.
Yet round our fea-girt fhore they rife in crowds :
What was the great Parnaffus' felf to thee,
Mount Skiddaw ?   In his natural fovereignty
Our Britifh hill is fairer far : he fhrouds
His double-fronted head in higher clouds,
And pours forth ftreams more fweet than Caftaly.

"*THE CHILDLESS FATHER.*"

" Up, Timothy, up, with your ſtaff, and away !
Not a ſoul in the village this morning will ſtay ;
The hare has juſt ſtarted from Hamilton's grounds,
And Skiddaw is glad with the cry of the hounds."

—Of coats and of jackets, grey, ſcarlet, and green,
On the ſlopes of the paſtures all colours were ſeen ;
With their comely blue aprons, and caps white as ſnow,
The girls on the hills made a holiday ſhow.

The baſin of boxwood, juſt ſix months before,
Had ſtood on the table at Timothy's door.
A coffin through Timothy's threſhold had paſſ'd ;
One child did it bear, and that child was his laſt.

Now faſt up the dell came the noiſe and the fray,
The horſe and the horn, and the " hark ! hark away ! "
Old Timothy took up his ſtaff, and he ſhut,
With a leiſurely motion, the door of his hut.

Perhaps to himfelf at that moment he faid,
" The key I muft take, for my Helen is dead."
But of this in my ears not a word did he fpeak,
And he went to the chafe with a tear on his cheek.

INSCRIPTION

For the Spot where the Hermitage Stood

ON ST. HERBERT'S ISLAND, DERWENT-WATER.

This ifland, guarded from profane approach
By mountains high, and waters widely fpread,
Is that recefs to which St. Herbert came
In life's decline: a felf-fecluded man,
After long exercife in focial cares
And offices humane, intent to adore
The Deity, with undiftracted mind,
And meditate on everlafting things.

—Stranger! this fhapelefs heap of ftones and earth
(Long be its moffy covering undifturbed !)
Is reverenced as a veftige of the abode

In which, through many feafons, from the world
Removed, and the affections of the world,
He dwelt in folitude.—But he had left
A fellow-labourer, whom the good man loved
As his own foul.   And when within his cave
Alone he knelt before the crucifix,
While o'er the Lake the cataract of Lodore
Pealed to his orifons, and when he paced
Along the beach of this fmall ifle, and thought
Of his companion, he would pray that both
(Now that their earthly duties were fulfilled)
Might die in the fame moment.   Nor in vain
So prayed he : as our chronicles report,
Though here the Hermit numbered his laft day,
Far from St. Cuthbert his beloved friend,
Thofe holy men both died in the fame hour.

Brougham Caſtle.

☙

SONG,

AT THE FEAST OF BROUGHAM CASTLE,

Upon the reſtoration of Lord Clifford, the Shepherd, to the Eſtates and Honours of his Anceſtors.

HIGH in the breathleſs hall the minſtrel ſate,
And Emont's murmur mingled with the ſong,—
    The words of ancient time I thus tranſlate,
    A feſtal ſtrain that hath been ſilent long :—

    " From town to town, from tower to tower,
  The red roſe is a gladſome flower.
  Her thirty years of winter paſt,
  The red roſe is revived at laſt ;
  She lifts her head for endleſs ſpring,
  For everlaſting bloſſoming :
  Both roſes flouriſh, red and white ;
  In love and ſiſterly delight,

The two that were at ſtrife are blended,
And all old troubles now are ended.—
Joy! joy to both! but moſt to her
Who is the flower of Lancaſter!
Behold her how ſhe ſmiles to-day
On this great throng, this bright array!
Fair greeting doth ſhe ſend to all
From every corner of the hall;
But, chiefly, from above the board
Where ſits in ſtate our rightful lord,
A Clifford to his own reſtored!

   " They came with banner, ſpear, and ſhield,
And it was proved in Boſworth-field.
Not long the avenger was withſtood—
Earth helped him with the cry of blood;
St. George was for us, and the might
Of bleſſed angels crowned the right.
Loud voice the land hath uttered forth,
We loudeſt in the faithful North:
Our fields rejoice, our mountains ring,
Our ſtreams proclaim a welcoming;
Our ſtrong abodes and caſtles ſee
The glory of their loyalty.
How glad is Skipton at this hour—
Though ſhe is but a lonely tower!
Silent, deſerted of her beſt,

Without an inmate or a gueſt,
Knight, ſquire, or yeoman, page or groom ;
We have them at the feaſt of Brough'm.
How glad Pendragon—though the ſleep
Of years be on her!—She ſhall reap
A taſte of this great pleaſure, viewing
As in a dream her own renewing.
Rejoiced is Brough, right glad I deem,
Beſide her little humble ſtream ;
And ſhe that keepeth watch and ward,
Her ſtatelier Eden's courſe to guard ;
They both are happy at this hour,
Though each is but a lonely tower :—
But here is perfect joy and pride
For one fair houſe by Emont's ſide,
This day diſtinguiſhed without peer ;
To ſee her maſter, and to cheer
Him and his lady mother dear !

" Oh ! it was a time forlorn,
When the fatherleſs was born—
Give her wings that ſhe may fly,
Or ſhe ſees her infant die !
Swords that are with ſlaughter wild
Hunt the mother and the child.
Who will take them from the light ?
—Yonder is a man in ſight—

Yonder is a houfe— but where ?
No, they muft not enter there.
To the caves, and to the brooks,
To the clouds of heaven fhe looks ;
She is fpeechlefs, but her eyes
Pray in ghoftly agonies.
Blifsful Mary, mother mild,
Maid and mother undefiled,
Save a mother and her child !

"Now who is he that bourds with joy
On Carrock's fide, a fhepherd-boy ?
No thoughts hath he but thoughts that pafs
Light as the wind along the grafs.
Can this be he who hither came
In fecret like a fmothered flame ?
O'er whom fuch thankful tears were fhed
For fhelter, and a poor man's bread !
God loves the child ; and God hath willed
That thofe dear words fhould be fulfilled,
The lady's words, when forced away,
The laft fhe to her babe did fay,
    My own, my own, thy fellow-gueft
I may not be ; but reft thee, reft,
For lowly fhepherd's life is beft !'
    " Alas ! when evil men are ftrong,
No life is good, no pleafure long.

The boy muſt part from Moſedale's groves,
And leave Blencathara's rugged coves,
And quit the flowers that Summer brings
To Glenderamakin's lofty ſprings ;
Muſt vaniſh, and his careleſs cheer
Be turned to heavineſs and fear.
--Give Sir Lancelot Threlkeld praiſe ;
Hear it, good man, old in days !
Thou tree of covert and of reſt
For this young bird that is diſtreſt ;
Among thy branches ſafe he lay,
And he was free to ſport and play
When falcons were abroad for prey.

" A recreant harp, that ſings of fear
And heavineſs in Clifford's ear !
I ſaid, when evil men are ſtrong,
No life is good, no pleaſure long, —
A weak and cowardly untruth !
Our Clifford was a happy youth,
And thankful through a weary time,
That brought him up to manhood's prime.
—Again he wanders forth at will,
And tends a flock from hill to hill :
His garb is humble; ne'er was ſeen
Such garb with ſuch a noble mien ;
Among the ſhepherd-grooms no mate

Hath he, a child of ſtrength and ſtate !
Yet lacks not friends for ſolemn glee,
And a cheerful company,
That learned of him ſubmiſſive ways,
And comforted his private days.
To his ſide the fallow-deer
Came, and reſted without fear ;
The eagle, lord of land and ſea,
Stooped down to pay him fealty ;
And both the undying fiſh that ſwim
Through Bowſcale-Tarn did wait on him ;
The pair were ſervants of his eye
In their immortality ;
They moved about in open ſight,
To and fro, for his delight.
He knew the rocks which angels haunt
On the mountains viſitant ;
He hath kenned them taking wing :
And the caves where fairies ſing
He hath entered ; and been told
By voices how men lived of old.
Among the heavens his eye can ſee
Face of thing that is to be ;
And, if men report him right,
He can whiſper words of might.
—Now another day is come,
Fitter hope and nobler doom :

He hath thrown afide his crook,
And hath buried deep his book ;
Armour rufting in his halls
On the blood of Clifford calls ;—
' Quell the Scot,' exclaims the Lance--
Bear me to the heart of France,
Is the longing of the Shield—
Tell thy name, thou trembling Field ;
Field of death, where'er thou be,
Groan thou with our victory !
Happy day, and mighty hour,
When our fhepherd, in his power,
Mailed and horfed, with lance and fword,
To his anceftors reftored,
Like a re appearing ftar,
Like a glory from afar,
Firft fhall head the flock of war!"

Alas ! the fervent harper did not know
    That for a tranquil foul the lay was framed,
Who, long compelled in humble walks to go,
    Was foftened into feeling, foothed, and tamed.

Love had he found in huts where poor men lie,
    His daily teachers had been woods and rills,
The filence that is in the ftarry fky,
    The fleep that is among the lonely hills.

In him the favage virtue of the race,
   Revenge, and all ferocious thoughts, were dead:
Nor did he change ; but kept in lofty place
   The wifdom which adverfity had bred.

Glad were the vales, and every cottage hearth ;
   The Shepherd-lord was honoured more and more :
And, ages after he was laid in earth,
   " The Good Lord Clifford" was the name he bore.

Black Comb.

STAY, bold adventurer! reſt awhile thy limbs
On this commodious ſeat; for much remains
Of hard aſcent before thou reach the top
Of this huge eminence,—from blackneſs named,
And, to far-travelled ſtorms of ſea and land,
A favourite ſpot of tournament and war!
But thee may no ſuch boiſterous viſitants
Moleſt; may gentle breezes fan thy brow;
And neither cloud conceal, nor miſty air
Bedim the grand terraqueous ſpectacle,
From centre to circumference unveiled!
Know, if thou grudge not to prolong thy reſt,
That, on the ſummit whither thou art bound,
A geographic labourer pitched his tent,

P

With books fupplied and inftruments of art,
To meafure height and diftance ; lonely tafk,
Week after week purfued !—To him was given
Full many a glimpfe (but fparingly beftowed
On timid man) of Nature's proceffes
Upon the exalted hills. He made report
That once, while there he plied his ftudious work
Within that canvas dwelling, fuddenly
The many-coloured map before his eyes
Became invifible : for all around
Had darknefs fallen—unthreatened, unproclaimed—
As if the golden day itfelf had been
Extinguifhed in a moment ; total gloom,
In which he fate alone, with unclofed eyes,
Upon the blinded mountain's filent top !

VIEW FROM THE TOP OF BLACK COMB.

This height a miniftering angel might feleēt :
For from the fummit of BLACK COMB (dread name
Derived from clouds and ftorms !) the ampleft range
Of unobftruēted profpeēt may be seen
That Britifh ground commands :—low dufky traēts
Where Trent is nurfed, far fouthward ! Cambrian Hills
To the fouth-weft, a multitudinous fhow ;
And, in a line of eye-fight linked with thefe,

The hoary peaks of Scotland that give birth
To Teviot's ſtream, to Annan, Tweed, and Clyde;—
Crowding the quarter whence the ſun comes forth,
Gigantic mountains rough with crags; beneath,
Right at the imperial ſtation's weſtern baſe,
Main ocean, breaking audibly, and ſtretched
Far into ſilent regions, blue and pale ;
And viſibly engirding Mona's Iſle
That, as we left the plain, before our ſight
Stood like a lofty mount, uplifting ſlowly
(Above the convex of the watery globe)
Into clear view the cultured fields that ſtreak
Its habitable ſhores ; but now appears
A dwindled objeƈt, and ſubmits to lie
At the ſpeƈtator's feet.—Yon azure ridge,
Is it a periſhable cloud—or there
Do we behold the frame of Erin's coaſt ?
Land ſometimes by the roving ſhepherd ſwain
(Like the bright confines of another world)
Not doubtfully perceived.—Look homeward now !
In depth, in height, in circuit, how ſerene
The ſpeƈtacle, how pure !—Of Nature's works,
In earth, and air, and earth-embracing ſea,
A revelation infinite it ſeems ;
Diſplay auguſt of man's inheritance,
Of Britain's calm felicity and power.

TO THE RIVER DUDDON.

O mountain ſtream ! the ſhepherd and his cot
Are privileged inmates of deep ſolitude:
Nor would the niceſt anchorite exclude
A field or two of brighter green, or plot
Of tillage-ground, that ſeemeth like a ſpot
Of ſtationary ſunſhine : thou haſt viewed
Theſe only, Duddon ! with their paths renewed
By fits and ſtarts, yet this contents thee not.
Thee hath ſome awful ſpirit impelled to leave,
Utterly to deſert the haunts of men.
Though ſimple thy companions were and few ;
And through this wilderneſs a paſſage cleave,
Attended but by thy own voice, ſave when
The clouds and fowls of the air thy way purſue.

The Brothers.

HESE tourifts, heaven preferve us! needs muft live
A profitable life : fome glance along,
Rapid and gay, as if the earth were air,
And they were butterflies to wheel about
Long as the Summer lafted : fome, as wife,
Upon the forehead of a jutting crag
Sit perched, with book and pencil on their knee,
And look and fcribble, fcribble on and look,
Until a man might travel twelve ftout miles,
Or reap an acre of his neighbour's corn.
But for that moping fon of idlenefs,
Why can he tarry *yonder?*—In our churchyard
Is neither epitaph nor monument,
Tombftone nor name—only the turf we tread
And a few natural graves." To Jane, his wife,
Thus fpake the homely Prieft of Ennerdale.
It was a July evening ; and he fate

Upon the long ftone-feat beneath the eaves
Of his old cottage,—as it chanced, that day,
Employed in winter's work.   Upon the ftone
His wife fate near him, teafing matted wool,
While, from the twin cards toothed with glittering wire,
He fed the fpindle of the youngeft child,
Who turned her large round wheel in the open air
With back and forward fteps.   Towards the field
In which the parifh chapel ftood alone,
Girt round with a bare ring of moffy wall,
While half an hour went by, the Prieft had fent
Many a long look of wonder : and at laft,
Rifen from his feat, befide the fnow-white ridge
Of carded wool which the old man had piled,
He laid his implements with gentle care,
Each in the other locked ; and, down the path
Which from his cottage to the churchyard led,
He took his way, impatient to accoft
The Stranger, whom he faw ftill lingering there.

'T was one well known to him in former days,
A fhepherd-lad :—who ere his fixteenth year
Had left that calling, tempted to entruft
His expectations to the fickle winds
And perilous waters,—with the mariners
A fellow-mariner,—and fo had fared
Through twenty feafons ; but he had been reared

Among the mountains, and he in his heart
Was half a shepherd on the stormy seas.
Oft in the piping shrouds had Leonard heard
The tones of waterfalls, and inland sounds
Of caves and trees:—and, when the regular wind
Between the tropics filled the steady sail,
And blew with the same breath through days and weeks,
Lengthening invisibly its weary line
Along the cloudless main, he, in those hours
Of tiresome indolence, would often hang
Over the vessel's side, and gaze and gaze ;
And, while the broad green wave and sparkling foam
Flashed round him images and hues that wrought
In union with the employment of his heart,
He, thus by feverish passion overcome,
Even with the organs of his bodily eye,
Below him, in the bosom of the deep,
Saw mountains—saw the forms of sheep that grazed
On verdant hills—with dwellings among trees,
And shepherds clad in the same country grey
Which he himself had worn.

                                And now at last
From perils manifold, with some small wealth
Acquired by traffic in the Indian Isles,
To his parental home he is returned,

With a determined purpofe to refume
The life which he lived there ; both for the fake
Of many darling pleafures, and the love
Which to an only brother he has borne
In all his hardfhips, fince that happy time
When, whether it blew foul or fair, they two
Were brother-fhepherds on their native hills.
—They were the laft of all their race : and now,
When Leonard had approached his home, his heart
Failed in him ; and, not venturing to inquire
Tidings of one whom he fo dearly loved,
Towards the churchyard he had turned afide,—
That, as he knew in what particular fpot
His family were laid, he thence might learn
If ftill his Brother lived, or to the file
Another grave was added.—He had found
Another grave,—near which a full half-hour
He had remained ; but, as he gazed, there grew
Such a confufion in his memory,
That he began to doubt ; and he had hopes
That he had feen this heap of turf before,—
That it was not another grave ; but one
He had forgotten.   He had loft his path,
As up the vale, that afternoon, he walked
Through fields which once had been well known to him :
And oh ! what joy the recollection now
Sent to his heart ! he lifted up his eyes,

And, looking round, imagined that he faw
Strange alteration wrought on every fide,
Among the woods and fields, and that the rocks
And the eternal hills themfelves were changed.

  By this the Prieft, who down the field had come
Unfeen by Leonard, at the churchyard gate
Stopped fhort,—and thence, at leifure, limb by limb
Perufed him with a gay complacency.
Ay, thought the Vicar, fmiling to himfelf,
'Tis one of thofe who needs muft leave the path
Of the world's bufinefs to go wild alone :
His arms have a perpetual holiday ;
The happy man will creep about the fields,
Following his fancies by the hour, to bring
Tears down his cheeks, or folitary fmiles
Into his face, until the fetting fun
Write fool upon his forehead.   Planted thus
Beneath a fhed that over-arched the gate
Of this rude churchyard, till the ftars appeared
The good man might have communed with himfelf,
But that the Stranger, who had left the grave,
Approached; he recognifed the Prieft at once,
And, after greetings interchanged, and given
By Leonard to the Vicar as to one
Unknown to him, this dialogue enfued.

Q

LEONARD.

You live, Sir, in thefe dales, a quiet life :
Your years make up one peaceful family ;
And who would grieve and fret, if, welcome come
And welcome gone, they are fo like each other,
They cannot be remembered ?   Scarce a funeral
Comes to this churchyard once in eighteen months ;
And yet, fome changes muſt take place among you :
And you who dwell here, even among thefe rocks
Can trace the finger of mortality,
And fee, that with our threefcore years and ten
We are not all that periſh.——I remember,
For many years ago I paſſed this road,
There was a foot-way all along the fields
By the brook-fide—'tis gone—and that dark cleft !
To me it does not feem to wear the face
Which then it had.

PRIEST.

          Nay, Sir, for aught I know,
That chafm is much the fame—

LEONARD.

          But, furely, yonder——

PRIEST.

Ay, there, indeed, your memory is a friend
That does not play you falfe.—On that tall pike
(It is the lonelieft place of all thefe hills)
There were two fprings which bubbled fide by fide,
As if they had been made that they might be
Companions for each other : ten years back,
Clofe to thofe brother fountains, the huge crag
Was rent with lightning, one is dead and gone,
The other, left behind, is flowing ftill.——
For accidents and changes fuch as thefe,
We want not ftore of them ;—a waterfpout
Will bring down half a mountain ; what a feaft
For folks that wander up and down like you,
To fee an acre's breadth of that wide cliff
One roaring cataract!—A fharp May ftorm
Will come with loads of January fnow,
And in one night fend twenty fcore of fheep
To feed the ravens ; or a fhepherd dies
By fome untoward death among the rocks :
The ice breaks up and fweeps away a bridge—
A wood is felled :—and then for our own homes !
A child is born or chriftened, a field ploughed,
A daughter fent to fervice, a web fpun,
The old houfe-clock is decked with a new face ;
And hence, fo far from wanting facts or dates
To chronicle the time, we all have here

A pair of diaries, one ferving, Sir,
For the whole dale, and one for each fire-fide—
Yours was a ftranger's judgment : for hiftorians,
Commend me to thefe valleys !

LEONARD.

          Yet your churchyard
Seems, if fuch freedom may be ufed with you,
To fay that you are heedlefs of the paft :
An orphan could not find his mother's grave :
Here's neither head nor foot-ftone, plate of brafs,
Crofsbones nor fkull,—type of our earthly ftate,
Or emblem of our hopes : the dead man's home
Is but a fellow to that pafture-field.

PRIEST.

Why, there, Sir, is a thought that's new to me !
The ftone-cutters, 'tis true, might beg their bread
If every Englifh churchyard were like ours ;
Yet your conclufion wanders from the truth :
We have no need of names and epitaphs ;
We talk about the dead by our fire-fides.
And then, for our immortal part ! *we* want
No fymbols, Sir, to tell us that plain tale :
The thought of death fits eafy on the man
Who has been born and dies among the mountains.

LEONARD.

Your dalefmen, then, do in each other's thoughts
Poffefs a kind of fecond life : no doubt
You, Sir, could help me to the hiftory
Of half thefe graves ?

PRIEST.

For eight-fcore winters paft,
With what I've witneffed, and with what I've heard,
Perhaps I might ; and, on a winter's evening,
If you were feated at my chimney's nook,
By turning o'er thefe hillocks one by one,
We two could travel, Sir, through a ftrange round ;
Yet all in the broad highway of the world.
Now there's a grave—your foot is half upon it—
It looks juft like the reft ; and yet that man
Died broken-hearted.

LEONARD.

'Tis a common cafe.
We'll take another : who is he that lies
Beneath yon ridge, the laft of thofe three graves ?
It touches on that piece of native rock
Left in the churchyard wall.

PRIEST.

That's Walter Ewbank.
He had as white a head and frefh a cheek
As ever were produced by youth and age
Engendering in the blood of hale fourfcore.
Through five long generations had the heart
Of Walter's forefathers o'erflowed the bounds
Of their inheritance, that fingle cottage—
You fee it yonder!—and thofe few green fields.
They toiled and wrought, and ftill, from fire to fon,
Each ftruggled, and each yielded as before
A little—yet a little—and old Walter,
They left to him the family heart, and land,
With other burthens than the crop it bore.
Year after year the old man ftill kept up
A cheerful mind,—and buffeted with bond,
Intereft, and mortgages; at laft he fank,
And went into his grave before his time.
Poor Walter! whether it was care that fpurred him,
God only knows, but to the very laft
He had the lighteft foot in Ennerdale :
His pace was never that of an old man :
I almoft fee him tripping down the path
With his two grandfons after him :—but you,
Unlefs our landlord be your hoft to-night,
Have far to travel,—and on thefe rough paths
Even in the longeft day of midfummer—

LEONARD.

But thoſe two orphans !

PRIEST.

Orphans !—Such they were —
Yet not while Walter lived :—for, though their parents
Lay buried ſide by ſide as now they lie,
The old man was a father to the boys,
Two fathers in one father : and if tears,
Shed when he talked of them where they were not,
And hauntings from the infirmity of love,
Are aught of what makes up a mother's heart,
This old man, in the day of his old age,
Was half a mother to them.—If you weep, Sir,
To hear a ſtranger talking about ſtrangers,
Heaven bleſs you when you are among your kindred!
Ay—you may turn that way—it is a grave
Which will bear looking at.

LEONARD.

Theſe boys—I hope
They loved this good old man ?—

PRIEST.

They did—and truly :
But that was what we almoſt overlooked,

They were fuch darlings of each other.   For,
Though from their cradles they had lived with Walter,
The only kinfman near them, and though he
Inclined to them by reafon of his age,
With a more fond familiar tendernefs,
They, notwithftanding, had much love to fpare,
And it all went into each other's hearts.
Leonard, the elder by juft eighteen months,
Was two years taller : 'twas a joy to fee,
To hear, to meet them!—From their houfe the fchool
Was diftant three fhort miles—and in the time
Of ftorm and thaw, when every water-courfe
And unbridged ftream, fuch as you may have noticed
Crofling our roads at every hundred fteps,
Was fwollen into a noify rivulet,
Would Leonard then, when elder boys perhaps
Remained at home, go ftaggering through the fords,
Bearing his Brother on his back.   I've feen him,
On windy days, in one of thofe ftray brooks,
Ay, more than once, I've feen him mid-leg deep,
Their two books lying both on a dry ftone
Upon the hither fide : and once I faid,
As I remember, looking round thefe rocks
And hills on which we all of us were born,
That God who made the great book of the world
Would blefs fuch piety—

LEONARD.

It may be then—-

PRIEST.

Never did worthier lads break Englifh bread ;
The fineft Sunday that the Autumn faw,
With all its mealy clufters of ripe nuts,
Could never keep thofe boys away from church,
Or tempt them to an hour of Sabbath breach.
Leonard and James ! I warrant, every corner
Among thefe rocks, and every hollow place
Where foot could come, to one or both of them
Was known as well as to the flowers that grow there.
Like roebucks they went bounding o'er the hills :
They played like two young ravens on the crags :
Then they could write—ay, and fpeak too, as well
As many of their betters ; and for Leonard !
The very night before he went away,
In my own houfe I put into his hand
A Bible, and I'd wager twenty pounds
That, if he is alive, he has it yet.

LEONARD.

It feems, thefe Brothers have not lived to be
A comfort to each other.—

R

PRIEST.

That they might
Live to fuch end, is what both old and young,
In this our valley, all of us have wifhed,
And what, for my part, I have often prayed :
But Leonard—

LEONARD.

Then James ftill is left among you ?

PRIEST.

'Tis of the elder Brother I am fpeaking :
They had an uncle ;—he was at that time
A thriving man, and trafficked on the feas :
And, but for that fame uncle, to this hour
Leonard had never handled rope or fhroud.
For the boy loved the life which we lead here ;
And, though of unripe years, a ftripling only,
His foul was knit to this his native foil.
But, as I faid, old Walter was too weak
To ftrive with fuch a torrent ; when he died,
The eftate and houfe were fold ; and all their fheep,
A pretty flock, and which, for aught I know,
Had clothed the Ewbanks for a thoufand years :—
Well—all was gone, and they were deftitute ;

And Leonard, chiefly for his Brother's fake,
Refolved to try his fortune on the feas.
'Tis now twelve years fince we had tidings from him.
If there was one among us who had heard
That Leonard Ewbank was come home again,
From the great Gavel, down by Leeza's banks,
And down the Enna, far as Egremont,
The day would be a very feftival;
And thofe two bells of ours, which there you fee—
Hanging in the open air—but, O good Sir!
This is fad talk—they'll never found for him—
Living or dead.—When laft we heard of him,
He was in flavery among the Moors
Upon the Barbary coaft.—'T was not a little
That would bring down his fpirit; and, no doubt,
Before it ended in his death, the youth
Was fadly croffed—Poor Leonard! when we parted,
He took me by the hand, and faid to me,
If ever the day came when he was rich,
He would return, and on his father's land
He would grow old among us.

LEONARD.

If that day
Should come, 'twould needs be a glad day for him;
He would himfelf, no doubt, be happy then
As any that fhould meet him—

PRIEST.

Happy! Sir---

LEONARD.

You faid his kindred all were in their graves,
And that he had one Brother—

PRIEST.

That is but
A fellow tale of forrow.   From his youth
James, though not fickly, yet was delicate;
And Leonard being always by his fide
Had done fo many offices about him,
That, though he was not of a timid nature,
Yet ftill the fpirit of a mountain boy
In him was fomewhat checked; and, when his Brother
Was gone to fea, and he was left alone,
The little colour that he had was foon
Stolen from his cheek; he drooped, and pined, and pined—

LEONARD.

But thefe are all the graves of full-grown men!

PRIEST.

Ay, Sir, that paffed away : we took him to us;
He was the child of all the dale—he lived
Three months with one, and fix months with another;

And wanted neither food, nor clothes, nor love :
And many, many happy days were his.
But, whether blithe or fad, 'tis my belief
His abfent Brother ftill was at his heart.
And, when he lived beneath our roof, we found
(A practice till this time unknown to him)
That often, rifing from his bed at night,
He in his fleep would walk about, and fleeping
He fought his Brother Leonard.—You are moved!
Forgive me, Sir : before I fpoke to you,
I judged you moft unkindly.

LEONARD.

       But this youth,
How did he die at laft ?

PRIEST.

     One fweet May morning,
(It will be twelve years fince when Spring returns,)
He had gone forth among the new-dropped lambs,
With two or three companions, whom it chanced
Some further bufinefs fummoned to a houfe
Which ftands at the dale-head. James, tired perhaps,
Or from fome other caufe, remained behind.
You fee yon precipice ;—it almoft looks
Like fome vaft building made of many crags ;
And in the midft is one particular rock

That rifes like a column from the vale,
Whence by our fhepherds it is called THE PILLAR.
James pointed to its fummit, over which
They all had purpofed to return together,
And told them that he there would wait for them ;
They parted, and his comrades paffed that way
Some two hours after, but they did not find him
Upon the fummit—at the appointed place.
Of this they took no heed : but one of them,
Going by chance at night into the houfe
Which at that time was James's home, there learned
That nobody had feen him all that day :
The morning came, and ftill he was unheard of:
The neighbours were alarmed, and to the brook
Some went, and fome towards the lake : ere noon
They found him at the foot of that fame rock—
Dead, and with mangled limbs. The third day after
I buried him, poor youth, and there he lies !

LEONARD.

And that, then, *is* his grave ?—Before his death
You fay that he faw many happy years ?

PRIEST.

Ay, that he did—

LEONARD.

And all went well with him—

PRIEST.

If he had one, the youth had twenty homes.

LEONARD.

And you believe, then, that his mind was eafy ?—

PRIEST.

Yes, long before he died, he found that time
Is a true friend to forrow ; and unlefs
His thoughts were turned on Leonard's lucklefs fortune,
He talked about him with a cheerful love.

LEONARD.

He could not come to an unhallowed end!

PRIEST.

Nay, God forbid !—You recollect I mentioned
A habit which difquietude and grief
Had brought upon him ; and we all conjectured
That, as the day was warm, he had lain down
Upon the grafs,—and, waiting for his comrades,
He there had fallen afleep ; that, in his fleep,
He to the margin of the precipice
Had walked, and from the fummit had fallen headlong.
And fo no doubt he perifhed : at the time
We guefs that in his hands he muft have had
His fhepherd's ftaff ; for midway in the cliff

It had been caught ; and there for many years
It hung—and mouldered there.

          The Prieſt here ended—
The Stranger would have thanked him, but he felt
A guſhing from his heart, that took away
The power of ſpeech.   Both left the ſpot in ſilence ;
And Leonard, when they reached the churchyard gate,
As the Prieſt lifted up the latch, turned round,—
And looking at the grave, he ſaid, " My Brother."
The Vicar did not hear the words : and now,
Pointing towards the cottage, he entreated
That Leonard would partake his homely fare :
The other thanked him with a fervent voice ;
But added, that, the evening being calm,
He would purſue his journey.   So they parted.
It was not long ere Leonard reached a grove
That overhung the road : he there ſtopped ſhort,
And, ſitting down beneath the trees, reviewed
All that the Prieſt had ſaid : his early years
Were with him in his heart : his cheriſhed hopes,
And thoughts which had been his an hour before,
All preſſed on him with ſuch a weight, that now,
This vale where he had been ſo happy, ſeemed
A place in which he could not bear to live :
So he relinquiſhed all his purpoſes.
He travelled on to Egremont : and thence,

That night he wrote a letter to the Prieſt,
Reminding him of what had paſſed between them;
And adding, with a hope to be forgiven,
That it was from the weakneſs of his heart
He had not dared to tell him who he was.

This done, he went on ſhipboard, and is now
A ſeaman, a grey-headed mariner.

Defcriptions of Scenery.

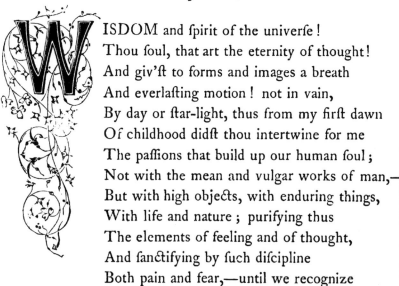

INFLUENCE OF NATURAL OBJECTS

*In calling forth and ftrengthening the Imagination in Boyhood and
Early Youth.*

ISDOM and fpirit of the univerfe!
Thou foul, that art the eternity of thought!
And giv'ft to forms and images a breath
And everlafting motion! not in vain,
By day or ftar-light, thus from my firft dawn
Of childhood didft thou intertwine for me
The paffions that build up our human foul;
Not with the mean and vulgar works of man,—
But with high objeéts, with enduring things,
With life and nature; purifying thus
The elements of feeling and of thought,
And fanétifying by fuch difcipline
Both pain and fear,—until we recognize
A grandeur in the beatings of the heart.

Nor was this fellowſhip vouchſafed to me
With ſtinted kindneſs. In November days,
When vapours rolling down the valleys made
A lonely ſcene more loneſome ; among woods
At noon ; and mid the calm of Summer nights,
When, by the margin of the trembling lake,
Beneath the gloomy hills, I homeward went
In ſolitude, ſuch intercourſe was mine :
'Twas mine among the fields both day and night,
And by the waters all the Summer long.
And in the froſty ſeaſon, when the ſun
Was ſet, and, viſible for many a mile,
The cottage windows through the twilight blazed,
I heeded not the ſummons :—happy time
It was, indeed, for all of us ; for me
It was a time of rapture !—Clear and loud
The village clock tolled ſix—I wheeled about,
Proud and exulting like an untired horſe
That cares not for its home.—All ſhod with ſteel
We hiſſed along the poliſhed ice, in games
Confederate, imitative of the chaſe
And woodland pleaſures,—the reſounding horn,
The pack loud-bellowing and the hunted hare.
So through the darkneſs and the cold we flew,
And not a voice was idle : with the din
Meanwhile the precipices rang aloud ;
The leafleſs trees and every icy crag

Tinkled like iron ; while the diftant hills
Into the tumult fent an alien found
Of melancholy, not unnoticed, while the ftars,
Eaftward, were fparkling clear, and in the weft
The orange fky of evening died away.

Not feldom from the uproar I retired
Into a filent bay, or fportively
Glanced fideway, leaving the tumultuous throng,
To cut acrofs the image of a ftar,
That gleamed upon the ice ; and oftentimes,
When we had given our bodies to the wind,
And all the fhadowy banks on either fide
Came fweeping through the darknefs, fpinning ftill
The rapid line of motion, then at once
Have I, reclining back upon my heels,
Stopped fhort ; yet ftill the folitary cliffs
Wheeled by me—even as if the earth had rolled
With vifible motion her diurnal round !
Behind me did they ftretch in folemn train,
Feebler and feebler, and I ftood and watched,
Till all was tranquil as a Summer fea.

A SUMMER FORENOON.

'Twas Summer, and the fun had mounted high :
Southward the landfcape indiftinctly glared
Through a pale fteam; but all the northern downs,
In cleareft air afcending, fhowed far off
A furface dappled o'er with fhadows flung
From many a brooding cloud, far as the fight
Could reach, thofe many fhadows lay in fpots
Determined and unmoved, with fteady beams
Of bright and pleafant funfhine interpofed ;
Pleafant to him who on the foft cool mofs
Extends his carelefs limbs along the front
Of fome huge cave, whofe rocky ceiling cafts
A twilight of its own, an ample fhade,
Where the wren warbles, while the dreaming man,
Half confcious of the foothing melody,
With fidelong eye looks out upon the fcene,
By that impending covert made more foft,
More low and diftant !   Other lot was mine,
Yet with good hope that foon I fhould obtain
As grateful refting-place and livelier joy.

From " The Excurfion," Book I.

LINES

Written while Sailing in a Boat at Evening.

How richly glows the water's breaſt
  Before us, tinged with Evening hues,
While, facing thus the crimſon weſt,
  The Boat her ſilent courſe purſues!
And ſee how dark the backward ſtream!
  A little moment paſt ſo ſmiling!
And ſtill, perhaps, with faithleſs gleam,
  Some other loiterers beguiling.

Such views the youthful Bard allure;
  But, heedleſs of the following gloom,
He deems their colours ſhall endure
  Till peace go with him to the tomb.
And let him nurſe his fond deceit,
  And what if he muſt die in ſorrow!
Who would not cheriſh dreams ſo ſweet,
  Though grief and pain may come to-morrow?

A NIGHT-PIECE.

————The ſky is overcaſt
With a continuous cloud of texture cloſe,
Heavy and wan, all whitened by the moon,
Which through that vale is indiſtinctly ſeen,
A dull, contracted circle, yielding light
So feebly ſpread that not a ſhadow falls,
Chequering the ground—from rock, plant, tree, or tower.
At length a pleaſant inſtantaneous gleam
Startles the penſive traveller as he treads
His loneſome path, with unobſerving eye
Bent earthwards ; he looks up—the clouds are ſplit
Aſunder,—and above his head he ſees
The clear moon, and the glory of the heavens.
There in a black blue vault ſhe ſails along,
Followed by multitudes of ſtars, that, ſmall
And ſharp, and bright, along the dark abyſs
Drive as ſhe drives ;—how faſt they wheel away,
Yet vaniſh not!—the wind is in the tree,
But they are ſilent ;—ſtill they roll along
Immeaſurably diſtant ;—and the vault,
Built round by thoſe white clouds, enormous clouds,
Still deepens its unfathomable depth.

At length the vifion clofes ; and the mind,
Not undifturbed by the delight it feels,
Which flowly fettles into peaceful calm,
Is left to mufe upon the folemn fcene.

NUTTING.

——It feems a day,
(I fpeak of one from many fingled out,)
One of thofe heavenly days that cannot die ;
When forth I fallied from our cottage-door,
With a huge wallet o'er my fhoulders flung,
A nutting-crook in hand, and turn'd my fteps
Towards the diftant woods, a figure quaint,
Tricked out in proud difguife of caft-off weeds
Which for that fervice had been hufbanded,
By exhortation of my frugal dame.
Motley accoutrement, of power to fmile
At thorns, and brakes, and brambles,—and, in truth,
More ragged than need was. Among the woods,
And o'er the pathlefs rocks, I forced my way,
Until, at length, I came to one dear nook
Unvifited, where not a broken bough
Drooped with its withered leaves, ungracious fign
Of devaftation, but the hazels rofe
Tall and erect, with milk-white clufters hung,

A virgin fcene!—A little while I ftood,
Breathing with fuch fuppreffion of the heart
As joy delights in ; and with wife reftraint
Voluptuous, fearlefs of a rival, eyed
The banquet,—or beneath the trees I fat
Among the flowers, and with the flowers I played ;
A temper known to thofe, who, after long
And weary expectation, have been bleffed
With fudden happinefs beyond all hope.—
Perhaps it was a bower beneath whofe leaves
The violets of five feafons re-appear·
And fade, unfeen by any human eye ;
Where fairy water-breaks do murmur on
For ever,—and I faw the fparkling foam,
And with my cheek on one of thofe green ftones
That, fleeced with mofs, beneath the fhady trees,
Lay round me, fcattered like a flock of fheep,—
I heard the murmur and the murmuring found,
In that fweet mood when pleafure loves to pay
Tribute to eafe ; and of its joy fecure,
The heart luxuriates with indifferent things,
Wafting its kindlinefs on ftocks and ftones,
And on the vacant air. Then up I rofe,
And dragged to earth both branch and bough, with crafh
And mercilefs ravage ; and the fhady nook
Of hazels, and the green and moffy bower,
Deformed and fullied, patiently gave up

T

Their quiet being; and, unlefs I now
Confound my prefent feelings with the paft,
Even then, when from the bower I turned away
Exulting, rich beyond the wealth of kings,
I felt a fenfe of pain when I beheld
The filent trees and the intruding fky.—
Then, deareft maiden! move along thefe fhades
In gentlenefs of heart; with gentle hand
Touch—for there is a fpirit in the woods.

LINES

Written in Early Spring.

I heard a thoufand blended notes,
    While in a grove I fat reclined,
In that fweet mood when pleafant thoughts
    Bring fad thoughts to the mind.

To her fair works did Nature link
    The human foul that through me ran ;
And much it grieved my heart to think
    What man has made of man.

Through primrofe tufts, in that fweet bower,
    The periwinkle trailed its wreaths ;
And 'tis my faith that every flower
    Enjoys the air it breathes.

The birds around me hopped and played,
　Their thoughts I cannot meafure :—
But the leaft motion which they made,
　It feemed a thrill of pleafure.

The budding twigs fpread out their fan,
　To catch the breezy air ;
And I muft think, do all I can,
　That there was pleafure there.

If I thefe thoughts may not prevent,
　If fuch be of my creed the plan,
Have I not reafon to lament
　What man has made of man ?

MY HEART LEAPS UP.

My heart leaps up when I behold
　A rainbow in the fky :
So was it when my life began ;
So is it now I am a man ;
　　So be it when I fhall grow old,
　　Or let me die !
The child is father of the man ;
And I could wifh my days to be
Bound each to each by natural piety.

YEW-TREES.

There is a Yew-tree, pride of Lorton Vale,
Which to this day ſtands ſingle, in the midſt
Of its own darkneſs, as it ſtood of yore,
Not loth to furniſh weapons for the bands
Of Umfraville or Percy, ere they marched
To Scotland's heaths ; or thoſe that croſſed the sea,
And drew their ſounding bows at Azincour,
Perhaps at earlier Crecy, or Poiĉtiers.
Of vaſt circumference and gloom profound
This ſolitary tree !—a living thing
Produced too ſlowly ever to decay ;
Of form and aſpeĉt too magnificent
To be deſtroyed.   But worthier ſtill of note
Are thoſe fraternal four of Borrowdale,
Joined in one ſolemn and capacious grove ;
Huge trunks !—and each particular trunk a growth
Of intertwiſted fibres ſerpentine
Up-coiling, and inveterately convolved,—
Nor uninformed with phantaſy, and looks
That threaten the profane ;—a pillared ſhade,
Upon whoſe graſſleſs floor of red-brown hue,
By ſheddings from the pining umbrage tinged
Perennially—beneath whoſe ſable roof
Of boughs, as if for feſtal purpoſe, decked
With unrejoicing berries, ghoſtly ſhapes

May meet at noontide—Fear and trembling Hope,
Silence and Forefight—Death the fkeleton
And Time the fhadow,—there to celebrate,
As in a natural temple fcattered o'er
With altars undifturbed of mofly ftone,
United worfhip; or in mute repofe
To lie, and liften to the mountain flood
Murmuring from Glaramara's inmoft caves.

SONNET TO A BROOK.

Brook! whofe fociety the Poet feeks,
Intent his wafted fpirits to renew;
And whom the curious painter doth purfue
Through rocky paffes, among flowery creeks,
And tracks thee dancing down thy water-breaks;
If I fome type of thee did wifh to view,
Thee,—and not thee thyfelf, I would not do
Like Grecian artifts, give thee human cheeks,
Channels for tears; no Naiad fhould'ft thou be,
Have neither limbs, feet, feathers, joints, nor hairs;
It feems the eternal foul is clothed in thee
With purer robes than thofe of flefh and blood,
And hath beftowed on thee a better good;
Unwearied joy, and life without its cares.

ADMONITION,

Intended more particularly for the perufal of thofe who may have happened to be enamoured of fome beautiful Place of Retreat in the Country of the Lakes.

Yes, there is holy pleafure in thine eye!
—The lovely cottage in the guardian nook
Hath ftirred thee deeply; with its own dear brook,
Its own fmall pafture, almoft its own fky!
But covet not the abode—Oh! do not figh,
As many do, repining while they look;
Sighing a wifh to tear from Nature's book
This blifsful leaf with harfh impiety.
Think what the home would be if it were thine,
Even thine, though few thy wants!—Roof, window, door,
The very flowers are facred to the poor,
The rofes to the porch which they entwine:
Yea, all, that now enchants thee, from the day
On which it fhould be touched, would melt, and melt
    away!

SONNETS.

"Beloved Vale!" I faid, "when I fhall con
Thofe many records of my childifh years,
Remembrance of myfelf and of my peers
Will prefs me down: to think of what is gone

Will be an awful thought, if life have one."
But, when into the Vale I came, no fears
Diftreffed me ; I looked round, I fhed no tears ;
Deep thought, or awful vifion, I had none.
By thoufand petty fancies I was croffed,
To fee the trees, which I had thought fo tall,
Mere dwarfs ; the brooks fo narrow, fields fo fmall.
A juggler's balls old Time about him toffed ;
I looked, I ftared, I fmiled, I laughed ; and all
The weight of fadnefs was in wonder loft.

The world is too much with us ; late and foon,
Getting and fpending, we lay wafte our powers :
Little we fee in Nature that is ours ;
We have given our hearts away, a fordid boon !
This fea that bares her bofom to the moon ;
The winds that will be howling at all hours,
And are up-gathered now like fleeping flowers ;
For this, for everything, we are out of tune ;
It moves us not.—Great God ! I'd rather be
A pagan fuckled in a creed outworn ;
So might I, ftanding on this pleafant lea,
Have glimpfes that would make me lefs forlorn ;
Have fight of Proteus rifing from the fea ;
Or hear old Triton blow his wreathed horn.

How fweet it is, when mother Fancy rocks
The wayward brain, to faunter through a wood !
An old place, full of many a lovely brood,
Tall trees, green arbours, and ground-flowers in flocks ;
And wild rofe tip-toe upon hawthorn ftocks,
Like to a bonny lafs, who plays her pranks
At wakes and fairs with wandering mountebanks,—
When fhe ftands crefting the clown's head, and mocks
The crowd beneath her.   Verily, I think,
Such place to me is fometimes like a dream,
Or map of the whole world : thoughts, link by link,
Enter through ears and eyefight, with fuch gleam
Of all things, that at laft in fear I fhrink,
And leap at once from the delicious ftream.

Mark the concentrated hazels that enclofe
Yon old grey Stone, protected from the ray
Of noontide funs :—and even the beams that play
And glance, while wantonly the rough wind blows,
Are feldom free to touch the mofs that grows
Upon that roof—amid embowering gloom
The very image framing of a tomb,
In which fome ancient chieftain finds repofe
Among the lonely mountains.—Live, ye trees !
And thou, grey Stone, the penfive likenefs keep

Of a dark chamber where the mighty fleep :
For more than fancy to the influence bends,
When folitary Nature condefcends
To mimic Time's forlorn humanities.

IT IS A BEAUTEOUS EVENING.

It is a beauteous evening, calm and free,
The holy time is quiet as a nun
Breathlefs with adoration ; the broad fun
Is finking down in its tranquillity ;
The gentlenefs of Heaven is on the fea :
Liften ! the mighty being is awake,
And doth with his eternal motion make
A found like thunder everlaftingly.
Dear child ! dear girl ! that walkeft with me here,
If thou appear'ft untouch'd by folemn thought,
Thy nature therefore is not lefs divine :
Thou lieft "in Abraham's bofom" all the year;
And worfhipp'ft at the temple's inner fhrine,
God being with thee when we know it not.

CALM IS ALL NATURE AS A RESTING WHEEL.

Calm is all nature as a refting wheel.
The kine are couch'd upon the dewy grafs ;
The horfe alone, feen dimly as I pafs,
Is cropping audibly his later meal :
Dark is the ground, a flumber feems to fteal
O'er vale, and mountain, and the ftarlefs fky,
Now, in this blank of things, a harmony,
Home-felt, and home-created, comes to heal
That grief for which the fenfes ftill fupply
Frefh food ; for only then, when memory
Is hufh'd, am I at reft.   My friends! reftrain
Thofe bufy cares that would allay my pain ;
Oh, leave me to myfelf! nor let me feel
The officious touch that makes me droop again.

Domeſtic Poems.

THE PET LAMB.

A PASTORAL.

THE dew was falling faſt, the ſtars began to blink;
  I heard a voice: it ſaid, "Drink, pretty creature,
    drink!"
And, looking o'er the hedge, before me I eſpied
  A ſnow-white mountain lamb, with a maiden at
    its ſide.

No other ſheep was near, the lamb was all alone,
And by a ſlender cord was tethered to a ſtone;
  With one knee on the graſs did the little maiden
    kneel,
  While to that mountain lamb ſhe gave its evening
    meal.

The lamb, while from her hand he thus his ſupper took,
Seemed to feaſt with head and ears, and his tail with pleaſure
  ſhook.
"Drink, pretty creature, drink," ſhe ſaid, in ſuch a tone
That I almoſt received her heart into my own.

'Twas little Barbara Lewthwaite, a child of beauty rare!
I watched them with delight ; they were a lovely pair.
Now, with her empty can the maiden turned away ;
But, ere ten yards were gone, her footſteps did ſhe ſtay.

Towards the lamb ſhe looked ; and from that ſhady place
I, unobſerved, could ſee the workings of her face :
If Nature to her tongue could meaſured numbers bring,
Thus, thought I, to her lamb that little maid might ſing :—

"What ails thee, young one ?   What ?   Why pull ſo at thy
    cord ?
Is it not well with thee ?   Well both for bed and board ?
Thy plot of graſs is ſoft, and green as graſs can be ;
Reſt, little young one, reſt ; what is't that aileth thee ?

"What is it thou would'ſt ſeek ?   What is wanting to thy
    heart ?
Thy limbs, are they not ſtrong ?   And beautiful thou art :
This graſs is tender graſs ; theſe flowers they have no peers ;
And that green corn, all day, is ruſtling in thy ears !

"If the ſun be ſhining hot, do but ſtretch thy woollen chain,
This beech is ſtanding by, its covert thou canſt gain ;
For rain and mountain ſtorms ! the like thou need'ſt not fear—
The rain and ſtorm are things which ſcarcely can come here.

" Reſt, little young one, reſt; thou haſt forgot the day
When my father found thee firſt in places far away:
Many flocks were on the hills, but thou wert owned by none,
And thy mother from thy ſide for evermore was gone.

" He took thee in his arms, and in pity brought thee home :
A bleſſed day for thee ! then whither would'ſt thou roam ?
A faithful nurſe thou haſt; the dam that did thee yean
Upon the mountain-tops no kinder could have been.

" Thou know'ſt that twice a day I have brought thee in this
        can
Freſh water from the brook, as clear as ever ran ;
And twice in the day, when the ground is wet with dew,
I bring thee draughts of milk, warm milk it is, and new.

" Thy limbs will ſhortly be twice as ſtout as they are now,
Then I'll yoke thee to my cart like a pony in the plough ;
My playmate thou ſhalt be ; and, when the wind is cold,
Our hearth ſhall be thy bed, our houſe ſhall be thy fold.

" It will not, will not reſt !—Poor creature, can it be
That 'tis thy mother's heart which is working ſo in thee ?
Things that I know not of, belike to thee are dear,
And dreams of things which thou can'ſt neither ſee nor hear.

" Alas, the mountain-tops that look fo green and fair !
I've heard of fearful winds and darknefs that come there ;
The little brooks that feem all paftime and all play,
When they are angry, roar like lions for their prey.

" Here thou need'ft not dread the raven in the fky ;
Night and day thou art fafe,--our cottage is hard by.
Why bleat fo after me ?   Why pull fo at thy chain ?
Sleep—and at break of day I will come to thee again ! "

—As homeward through the lane I went with lazy feet,
This fong to myfelf did I oftentimes repeat ;
And it feemed, as I retraced the ballad line by line,
That but half of it was hers, and one-half of it was *mine.*

Again, and once again did I repeat the fong ;
" Nay," faid I, " more than half to the *damfel* muft belong,
For fhe looked with fuch a look, and fhe fpake with fuch a
     tone,
That I almoft received her heart into my own."

LUCY GRAY;

OR SOLITUDE.

Oft I had heard of Lucy Gray ;
     And when I croffed the wild,
I chanced to fee at break of day
     The folitary child.

No mate, no comrade Lucy knew,
  She dwelt on a wild moor,
The fweeteft thing that ever grew
  Befide a human door.

You yet may fpy the fawn at play,
  The hare upon the green ;
But the fweet face of Lucy Gray
  Will never more be feen.

"To-night will be a ftormy night—
  You to the town muft go ;
And take a lantern, child, to light
  Your mother through the fnow."

"That, father, I will gladly do ;
  'Tis fcarcely afternoon—
The minfter clock has juft ftruck two,
  And yonder is the moon."

At this the father raifed his hook,
  And fnapped a faggot-band ;
He plied his work ;—and Lucy took
  The lantern in her hand.

Not blither is the mountain roe :
  With many a wanton ftroke
Her feet difperfe the powdery fnow,
  That rifes up like fmoke.

The ſtorm came on before its time :
  She wandered up and down ;
And many a hill did Lucy climb ;
  But never reached the town.

The wretched parents all that night
  Went ſhouting far and wide ;
But there was neither found nor ſight
  To ſerve them for a guide.

At day-break on a hill they ſtood
  That overlooked the moor ;
And thence they ſaw the bridge of wood,
  A furlong from their door.

And, turning homeward, now they cried,
  "In heaven we all ſhall meet !"
When in the ſnow the mother ſpied
  The print of Lucy's feet.

Then downward from the ſteep hill's edge
  They tracked the footmarks ſmall :
And through the broken hawthorn hedge,
  And by the long ſtone wall :

And then an open field they croſſed :
  The marks were ſtill the ſame ;
They tracked them on, nor ever loſt ;
  And to the bridge they came.

They followed from the fnowy bank
  The footmarks one by one,
Into the middle of the plank ;   .
  And further there were none !

Yet fome maintain that to this day
  She is a living child :
That you may fee fweet Lucy Gray
  Upon the lonefome wild.

O'er rough and fmooth fhe trips along,
  And never looks behind ;
And fings a folitary fong
  That whiftles in the wind.

THREE YEARS SHE GREW IN SUN AND SHOWER.

Three years fhe grew in fun and fhower,
Then Nature faid " a lovelier flower
On earth was never fown ;
This child I to myfelf will take :
She fhall be mine, and I will make
A lady of my own.

x

" Myfelf will to my darling be
Both law and impulfe ; and with me
The girl, in rock and plain,
In earth and heaven, in glade and bower,
Shall feel an overfeeing power
To kindle or reftrain.

" She fhall be fportive as the fawn,
That wild with glee acrofs the lawn
Or up the mountain fprings ;
And hers fhall be the breathing balm,
And hers the filence and the calm
Of mute infenfate things.

" The floating clouds their ftate fhall lend
To her ; for her the willow bend ;
Nor fhall fhe fail to fee
E'en in the motions of the ftorm
Grace that fhall mould the maiden's form
By filent fympathy.

" The ftars of midnight fhall be clear
To her ; and fhe fhall lean her ear
In many a fecret place
Where rivulets dance their wayward round,
And beauty born of murmuring found
Shall pafs into her face.

"And vital feelings of delight
Shall rear her form to ſtately height,
Her virgin boſom ſwell ;
Such thoughts to Lucy I will give
While ſhe and I together live
Here in this happy dell."

Thus Nature ſpake. The work was done—
How ſoon my Lucy's race was run !
She died, and left to me
This heath, this calm and quiet ſcene ;
The memory of what has been,
And never more will be.

SHE WAS A PHANTOM OF DELIGHT.

She was a phantom of delight
When firſt ſhe gleam'd upon my ſight ;
A lovely apparition, ſent
To be a moment's ornament ;
Her eyes as ſtars of twilight fair,
Like twilight's, too, her duſky hair ;
But all things elſe about her drawn
From May-time and the cheerful dawn ;

A dancing fhape, an image gay,
To haunt, to ftartle, and waylay.

I faw her upon nearer view,
A fpirit, yet a woman too !
Her houfehold motions light and free,
And fteps of virgin liberty;
A countenance in which did meet
Sweet records, promifes as fweet :
A creature not too bright or good
For human nature's daily food,
For tranfient forrows, fimple wiles,
Praife, blame, love, kiffes, tears, and fmiles.

And now I fee with eye ferene
The very pulfe of the machine ;
A being breathing thoughtful breath,
A traveller betwixt life and death ;
The reafon firm, the temperate will,
Endurance, forefight, ftrength, and fkill ;
A perfect woman, nobly plann'd,
To warn. to comfort, and command ;
And yet a fpirit ftill, and bright
With fomething of an angel light.

Poems on Flowers.

TO THE DAISY.

IN youth from rock to rock I went,
From hill to hill in difcontent,
Of pleafure high and turbulent,
　　　Moft pleafed when moft uneafy;
But now my own delights I make,—
My thirft at every rill can flake,—
And gladly Nature's love partake
　　　Of thee, fweet Daify!

When foothed a while by milder airs,
Thee Winter in the garland wears
That thinly fhades his few grey hairs;
　　　Spring cannot fhun thee;
While fummer fields are thine by right;
And Autumn, melancholy wight!
Doth in thy crimfon head delight,
　　　When rains are on thee.

In fhoals and bands, a morrice train,
Thou greet'ft the traveller in the lane ;
If welcomed once thou count'ft it gain ;
    Thou art not daunted,
Nor car'ft if thou be fet at naught :
And oft alone in nooks remote
We meet thee, like a pleafant thought
    When fuch are wanted.

Be violets in their fecret mews
The flowers the wanton zephyrs choofe ;
Proud be the rofe, with rains and dews
    Her head impearling ;
Thou liv'ft with lefs ambitious aim,
Yet haft not gone without thy fame ;
Thou art indeed by many a claim
    The poet's darling.

If to a rock from rains he fly,
Or, fome bright day of April fky,
Imprifoned by hot funfhine lie
    Near the green holly,
And wearily at length fhould fare ;
He need but look about, and there
Thou art ! a friend at hand to fcare
    His melancholy.

A hundred times, by rock or bower,
Ere thus I have lain couched an hour,
Have I derived from thy fweet power
    Some apprehenfion ;
Some fteady love ; fome brief delight ;
Some memory that had taken flight ;
Some chime of fancy, wrong or right ;
    Or ftray invention.

If ftately paffions in me burn,
And one chance look to thee fhould turn,
I drink out of an humbler urn
    A lowlier pleafure ;
The homely fympathy that heeds
The common life our nature breeds ;
A wifdom fitted to the needs
    Of hearts at leifure.

When fmitten by the morning ray,
I fee thee rife, alert and gay,
Then, cheerful flower ! my fpirits play
    With kindred gladnefs :
And when, at dufk, by dews oppreft
Thou fink'ft, the image of thy reft
Hath often eafed my penfive breaft
    Of careful fadnefs.

And all day long I number yet,
All feafons through, another debt,
Which I, wherever thou art met,
          To thee am owing;
An inftinct call it, a blind fenfe;
A happy, genial influence,
Coming one knows not how, nor whence,
          Nor whither going.

Child of the year ! that round doft run
Thy courfe, bold lover of the fun,
And cheerful when the day's begun
          As morning leveret,
Thy long-loft praife thou fhalt regain :
Dear thou fhalt be to future men
As in old time ;—thou not in vain
          Art Nature's favourite.

———

TO THE SAME FLOWER.

Bright flower ! whofe home is everywhere,
A pilgrim bold in Nature's care,
And all the long year through, the heir
          Of joy or forrow,

Methinks that there abides in thee
Some concord with humanity,
Given to no other flower I fee
    The foreſt thorough !

Is it that man is foon depreſſed ?
A thoughtlefs thing ! who, once unbleſſed,
Does little on his memory reſt,
    Or on his reafon ;
And thou would'ſt teach him how to find
A ſhelter under every wind,
A hope for times that are unkind
    And every feafon ?

Thou wandereſt the wide world about,
Unchecked by bride or fcrupulous doubt,
With friends to greet thee, or without,
    Yet pleafed and willing ;
Meek, yielding to the occafion's call,
And all things fuffering from all,
Thy function apoſtolical
    In peace fulfilling.

Y

TO THE SMALL CELANDINE ;

OR, COMMON PILEWORT.

Panfies, lilies, kingcups, daifies,
Let them live upon their praifes ;
Long as there's a fun that fets,
Primrofes will have their glory ;
Long as there are violets,
They will have a place in ftory :
There's a flower that fhall be mine,
'Tis the little Celandine.

Eyes of fome men travel far
For the finding of a ftar ;
Up and down the heavens they go,
Men that keep a mighty rout !
I'm as great as they, I trow,
Since the day I found thee out,
Little flower !—I'll make a ftir,
Like a great aftronomer.

Modeſt, yet withal an elf
Bold, and laviſh of thyſelf :
Since we needs muſt firſt have met,
I have ſeen thee, high and low,
Thirty years or more, and yet
'Twas a face I did not know ;
Thou haſt now, go where I may,
Fifty greetings in a day.

Ere a leaf is on a buſh,
In the time before the thruſh
Has a thought about its neſt,
Thou wilt come with half a call,
Spreading out thy gloſſy breaſt
Like a careleſs prodigal ;
Telling tales about the ſun,
When we've little warmth or none.

Poets, vain men in their mood !
Travel with the multitude ;
Never heed them ; I aver
That they all are wanton wooers ;
But the thrifty cottager,
Who ſtirs little out of doors,
Joys to ſpy thee near her home ;
Spring is coming, thou art come !

Comfort have thou of thy merit,
Kindly, unaffuming fpirit !
Carelefs of thy neighbourhood,
Thou doft fhow thy pleafant face
On the moor, and in the wood,
In the lane—there's not a place,
Howfoever mean it be,
But 't is good enough for thee.

Ill befall the yellow flowers,
Children of the flaring hours !
Buttercups, that will be feen,
Whether we will fee or no ;
Others, too, of lofty mien ;
They have done as worldlings do,
Taken praife that fhould be thine,
Little, humble Celandine !

Prophet of delight and mirth,
Scorned and flighted upon earth !
Herald of a mighty band,
Of a joyous train enfuing,
Singing at my heart's command,
In the lanes my thoughts purfuing,
I will fing, as doth behove,
Hymns in praife of what I love !

TO THE SAME FLOWER.

Pleafures newly found are fweet,
When they lie about our feet :
February laft, my heart
Firft at fight of thee was glad ;
All unheard of as thou art,
Thou muft needs, I think, have had,
Celandine ! and long ago,
Praife of which I nothing know.

I have not a doubt but he,
Whofoe'er the man might be,
Who the firft with pointed rays,
(Workman worthy to be fainted)
Set the fign-board in a blaze,
When the rifen fun he painted,
Took the fancy from a glance
At thy glittering countenance.

Soon as gentle breezes bring
News of winter's vanifhing,
And the children build their bowers,
Sticking kerchief-pots of mould

All about with full-blown flowers,
Thick as fheep in fhepherd's fold !
With the proudeft thou art there,
Mantling in the tiny fquare.

Often have I figh'd to meafure
By myfelf a lonely pleafure,
Sigh'd to think I read a book,
Only read, perhaps, by me ;
Yet I long could overlook
Thy bright coronet and thee,
And thy arch and wily ways,
And thy ftore of other praife.

Blithe of heart, from week to week,
Thou doft play at hide-and-feek ;
While the patient primrofe fits
Like a beggar in the cold,
Thou, a flower of wifer wits,
Slipp'ft into thy fhelter'd hold ;
Bright as any of the train,
When ye all are out again.

Thou art not beyond the moon,
But a thing " beneath our fhoon : "
Let, as old Magellan did,
Others roam about the fea ;

Build who will a pyramid;
Praife it is enough for me,
If there be but three or four
Who will love my little flower.

DAFFODILS.

I wandered lonely as a cloud
  That floats on high o'er vales and hills
When all at once I faw a crowd,
  A hoft of golden daffodils;
Befide the lake, beneath the trees,
Fluttering and dancing in the breeze.

Continuous as the ftars that fhine
  And twinkle on the milky way,
They ftretched in never-ending line
  Along the margin of a bay :
Ten thoufand faw I at a glance,
Toffing their heads in fprightly dance.

The waves befide them danced, but they
  Outdid the fparkling waves in glee :—
A Poet could not but be gay,
  In fuch a jocund company :

I gazed—and gazed—but little thought
What wealth the fhow to me had brought :

For oft when on my couch I lie,
      In vacant or in penfive mood,
They flafh upon that inward eye
      Which is the blifs of folitude,
And then my heart with pleafure fills,
And dances with the daffodils.

TO THE ROCK IN THE ORCHARD.

Who fancied what a pretty fight
This rock would be if edged around
With living fnowdrops—circlet bright ?
How glorious to this orchard ground !
Who loved the little rock, and fet
Upon its head this coronet ?

Was it the humour of a child ?
Or rather of fome love-fick maid,
Whofe brows, the day that fhe was ftyled
The fhepherd queen, were thus array'd !
Of man mature, or matron fage !
Or old man toying with his age ?

I afk'd—'twas whifper'd, the device
To each or all might well belong;
It is the fpirit of paradife
That prompts fuch work, a fpirit ftrong,
That gives to all the felf-fame bent
Where life is wife and innocent.

THE WATERFALL AND THE EGLANTINE.

" Begone, thou fond prefumptuous elf,"
    Exclaimed a thundering voice,
" Nor dare to thruft thy foolifh felf
    Between me and my choice!"
A falling Water, fwollen with fnows,
Thus fpake to a poor Briar-rofe,
    That, all befpattered with his foam,
And dancing high and dancing low,
Was living, as a child might know,
    In an unhappy home.

" Doft thou prefume my courfe to block?
    Off, off! or, puny thing!
I'll hurl thee headlong with the rock
    To which thy fibres cling."

z

The flood was tyrannous and ftrong ;
The patient Briar fuffered long,
    Nor did he utter groan or figh,
Hoping the danger would be paft :
But, feeing no relief, at laft
    He ventured to reply.

" Ah ! " faid the Briar, " blame me not ;
    Why fhould we dwell in ftrife ?
We who in this, our natal fpot,
    Once lived a happy life !
You ftirred me on my rocky bed—
What pleafure through my veins you fpread !
    The Summer long, from day to day,
My leaves you frefhened and bedewed ;
Nor was it common gratitude
    That did your cares repay.

" When Spring came on with bud and bell,
    Among thefe rocks did I
Before you hang my wreaths, to tell
    That gentle days were nigh !
And in the fultry Summer hours,
I fheltered you with leaves and flowers ;

And in my leaves—now fhed and gone—
The linnet lodged, and for us two
Chaunted his pretty fongs, when you
    Had little voice, or none.

" But now proud thoughts are in your breaft—
    What grief is mine you fee.
Ah! would you think, even yet, how bleft
    Together we might be !
Though of both leaf and flower bereft,
Some ornaments to me are left—
    Rich ftore of fcarlet hips is mine,
With which I, in my humble way,
Would deck you many a Winter's day,
    A happy Eglantine ! "

What more he faid I cannot tell,
The Torrent thundered down the dell
    With unabating hafte ;
I liftened, nor aught elfe could hear ;
The Briar quaked—and much I fear
    Thofe accents were his laft.

THE OAK AND THE BROOM.

A PASTORAL.

His fimple truths did Andrew glean
    Befide the babbling rills;
A careful ftudent he had been
    Among the woods and hills.
One Winter's night, when through the trees
The wind was thundering, on his knees
    His youngeft born did Andrew hold:
And while the reft, a ruddy quire,
Were feated round their blazing fire,
    This tale the fhepherd told:—

" I faw a crag, a lofty ftone
    As ever tempeft beat!
Out of its head an Oak had grown,
    A Broom out of its feet.
The time was March, a cheerful noon—
The thaw-wind, with the breath of June,
    Breathed gently from the warm fouth-weft:
When, in a voice fedate with age,
This Oak, a giant and a fage,
    His neighbour thus addreffed:

" Eight weary weeks through rock and clay,
　　Along this mountain's edge,
The froſt hath wrought both night and day,
　　Wedge driving after wedge.
Look up ! and think, above your head
What trouble, ſurely, will be bred ;
　　Laſt night I heard a craſh—'tis true,
The ſplinters took another road —
I ſee them yonder—what a load
　　For ſuch a thing as you !

" You are preparing, as before,
　　To deck your ſlender ſhape ;
And yet, juſt three years back—no more—
　　You had a ſtrange eſcape.
Down from yon cliff a fragment broke ;
It came, you know, with fire and ſmoke,
　　And hitherward it bent its way :
This ponderous block was caught by me,
And o'er your head, as you may ſee,
　　'T is hanging to this day !

" The thing had better been aſleep,
　　Whatever thing it were,
Or breeze, or bird, or dog, or ſheep,
　　That firſt did plant you there.

For you and your green twigs decoy
The little witlefs fhepherd-boy
   To come and flumber in your bower ;
And, truft me, on fome fultry noon,
Both you and he, Heaven knows how foon !
   Will perifh in one hour.

" From me this friendly warning take' —
   The Broom began to doze,
And thus, to keep herfelf awake,
   Did gently interpofe :
' My thanks for your difcourfe are due ;
That it is true, and more than true,
   I know, and I have known it long ;
Frail is the bond by which we hold
Our being, be we young or old,
   Wife, foolifh, weak, or ftrong.

" Difafters, do the beft we can,
   Will reach both great and fmall ;
And he is oft the wifeft man,
   Who is not wife at all.
For me, why fhould I wifh to roam ?
This fpot is my paternal home,
   It is my pleafant heritage ;
My father, many a happy year,
Here fpread his carelefs bloffoms, here
   Attained a good old age.

" Even fuch as his may be my lot :
    What caufe have I to haunt
My heart with terrors ?   Am I not
    In truth a favoured plant !
On me fuch bounty Summer pours,
That I am covered o'er with flowers;
    And, when the froft is in the fky,
My branches are fo frefh and gay,
That you might look at me and fay,
    This plant can never die.

" The butterfly, all green and gold,
    To me hath often flown,
Here in my bloffoms to behold
    Wings lovely as his own.
When grafs is chill with rain or dew,
Beneath my fhade the mother-ewe
    Lies with her infant lamb ; I fee
The love they to each other make,
And the fweet joy which they partake,
    It is a joy to me.'

" Her voice was blithe, her heart was light ;
    The Broom might have purfued
Her fpeech, until the ftars of night
    Their journey had renewed :
But in the branches of the Oak
Two ravens now began to croak

Their nuptial fong, a gladfome air :
And to her own green bower the breeze
That inftant brought two ftripling bees
    To reft and murmur there.

" One night, my children ! from the North
    There came a furious blaft ;
At break of day I ventured forth,
    And near the cliff I paffed.
The ftorm had fallen upon the Oak
And ftruck him with a mighty ftroke,
    And whirled, and whirled him far away ;
And in one hofpitable cleft
The little carelefs Broom was left
    To live for many a day."

Poems on Birds.

THE GREEN LINNET.

ENEATH thefe fruit-tree boughs that fhed
Their fnow-white bloffoms on my head,
With brighteft funfhine round me fpread
  Of Spring's unclouded weather,
In this fequeftered nook how fweet
To fit upon my orchard-feat!
And flowers and birds once more to greet,
  My laft year's friends together.

One have I marked, the happieft gueft
In all this covert of the bleft:
Hail to thee, far above the reft
  In joy of voice and pinion!
Thou, Linnet, in thy green array,
Prefiding fpirit here to-day,
Doft lead the revels of the May,
  And this is thy dominion.

While birds, and butterflies, and flowers,
Make all one band of paramours,
Thou, ranging up and down the bowers,
    Art fole in thy employment ;
A life, a prefence like the air,
Scattering thy gladnefs without care,
Too bleft with any one to pair,
    Thyfelf thy own enjoyment.

Upon ycn tuft of hazel trees,
That twinkle to the gufty breeze,
Behold him perched in ecftacies,
    Yet feeming ftill to hover ;
There ! where the flutter of his wings
Upon his back and body flings
Shadows and funny glimmerings,
    That cover him all over.

While thus before my eyes he gleams,
A brother of the leaves he feems ;
When in a moment forth he teems
    His little fong in gufhes :
As if it pleafed him to difdain
And mock the form which he did feign
While he was dancing with the train
    Of leaves among the bufhes.

TO A SKY-LARK.

Up with me ! up with me into the clouds !
  For thy fong, Lark, is ftrong ;
Up with me, up with me into the clouds !
    Singing, finging,
With all the heavens about thee ringing,
  Lift me, guide me till I find
That fpot which feems fo to thy mind !
I have walked through wildernelfes dreary,
  And to-day my heart is weary ;
  Had I now the wings of a faery,
    Up to thee would I fly.
There is madnefs about thee, and joy divine
    In that fong of thine :
Up with me, up with me, high and high,
To thy banqueting-place in the fky !
    Joyous as morning,
  Thou art laughing and fcorning :
Thou haft a neft for thy love and thy reft :
And, though little troubled with floth,
Drunken Lark ! thou would'ft be loth
To be fuch a traveller as I.
    Happy, happy liver !
With a foul as ftrong as a mountain river,
Pouring out praife to the Almighty giver,

Joy and jollity be with us both!
Hearing thee, or elfe fome other,
    As merry a brother,
I on the earth will go plodding on,
By myfelf, cheerfully, till the day is done.

TO THE CUCKOO.

O blithe new-comer! I have heard,
    I hear thee and rejoice:
O Cuckoo! fhall I call thee bird,
    Or but a wandering voice?

While I am lying on the grafs,
    Thy loud note fmites my ear!
From hill to hill it feems to pafs,
    At once far off and near!

I hear thee babbling to the vale
    Of funfhine and of flowers;
And unto me thou bring'ft a tale
    Of vifionary hours.

Thrice welcome, darling of the Spring!
    Even yet thou art to me
No bird, but an invifible thing,
    A voice, a myftery;

The fame whom in my fchool-boy days
   I liftened to ; that cry
Which made me look a thoufand ways
   In bufh, and tree, and fky.

To feek thee did I often rove
   Through woods and on the green ;
And thou wert ftill a hope, a love ;
   Still longed for, never feen !

And I can liften to thee yet ;
   Can lie upon the plain
And liften, till I do beget
   That golden time again.

O bleffed bird ! the earth we pace
   Again appears to be
An unfubftantial, faery place ;
   That is fit home for thee !

TO A NIGHTINGALE.

O Nightingale ! thou furely art
A creature of a fiery heart :—
Thefe notes of thine—they pierce and pierce ;
Tumultuous harmony and fierce !

Thou fing'ft as if the god of wine
Had helped thee to a valentine ;
A fong in mockery and defpite
Of fhades and dews and filent night,
And fteady blifs, and all the loves
Now fleeping in thefe peaceful groves.

I heard a ftock-dove fing or fay
His homely tale, this very day ;
His voice was buried among trees,
Yet to be come at by the breeze :
He did not ceafe ; but cooed—and cooed ;
And fomewhat penfively he wooed :
He fang of love with quiet blending,
Slow to begin, and never ending ;
Of ferious faith and inward glee :
That was the fong—the fong for me !

THE SPARROW'S NEST.

Behold, within the leafy fhade,
Thofe bright blue eggs together laid !
On me the chance-difcover'd fight
Gleam'd like a vifion of delight.—

I ſtarted—ſeeming to eſpy
The home and ſhelter'd bed,—
The ſparrow's dwelling which, hard by
My father's houſe, in wet or dry,
My ſiſter Emmeline and I
    Together viſited.

She look'd at it as if ſhe fear'd it ;
Still wiſhing, dreading to be near it :
Such heart was in her, being then
A little prattler among men.
The bleſſing of my later years
Was with me when a boy ;
She gave me eyes, ſhe gave me ears ;
And humble cares, and delicate fears ;
A heart, the fountain of ſweet tears ;
    And love, and thought, and joy.

Intimations of Immortality

FROM RECOLLECTIONS OF EARLY CHILDHOOD

The child is father of the man ;
And I could wish my days to be
Bound each to each by natural piety.

THERE was a time when meadow, grove, and
stream,
The earth, and every common fight,
To me did feem
Appareled in celeftial light,
The glory and the frefhnefs of a dream.
It is not now as it has been of yore ;—
Turn wherefoe'er I may,
By night or day,
The things which I have feen I now can fee no
more !

The rainbow comes and goes,
And lovely is the rofe ;—

The moon doth with delight
Look round her when the heavens are bare ;
Waters on a ſtarry night
Are beautiful and fair ;
The ſunſhine is a glorious birth ;
But yet I know, where'er I go,
That there hath paſſed away a glory from the earth.

Now, while the birds thus ſing a joyous ſong,
And while the young lambs bound
As to the tabor's ſound,
To me alone there came a thought of grief :
A timely utterance gave that thought relief,
And I again am ſtrong.
The cataracts blow their trumpets from the ſteep,—
No more ſhall grief of mine the ſeaſon wrong :
I hear the echoes through the mountains throng,
The winds come to me from the fields of ſleep,
And all the earth is gay ;
Land and ſea
Give themſelves up to jollity,
And with the heart of May
Doth every beaſt keep holiday ;—
Thou child of joy,
Shout round me, let me hear thy ſhouts, thou happy
Shepherd-boy !

Ye bleſſed creatures, I have heard the call
       Ye to each other make ; I ſee
The heavens laugh with you in your jubilee ;
       My heart is at your feſtival,
          My head hath its coronal,
The fulneſs of your bliſs I feel—I feel it all.
          Oh evil day ! if I were ſullen
          While earth herſelf is adorning,
             This ſweet May morning ;
          And the children are culling,
             On every ſide,
          In a thouſand valleys far and wide,
          Freſh flowers ; while the ſun ſhines warm,
And the babe leaps up on his mother's arm :—
          I hear, I hear, with joy I hear !
          —But there's a tree, of many one,
       A ſingle field which I have looked upon,
       Both of them ſpeak of ſomething that is gone :
             The panſy at my feet
             Doth the ſame tale repeat :
Whither is fled the viſionary gleam ?
Where is it now, the glory and the dream ?

Our birth is but a ſleep and a forgetting :
The ſoul that riſes with us, our life's ſtar,
          Hath had elſewhere its ſetting,
             And cometh from afar ;

Not in entire forgetfulnefs,
And not in utter nakednefs,
But trailing clouds of glory do we come
From God, who is our home :
Heaven lies about us in our infancy !
Shades of the prifon-houfe begin to clofe
Upon the growing boy,
But he beholds the light, and whence it flows,
He fees it in his joy ;
The youth, who daily farther from the eaft
Muft travel, ftill is Nature's prieft,
And by the vifion fplendid
Is on his way attended ;
At length the man perceives it die away,
And fade into the light of common day.

Earth fills her lap with pleafures of her own ;
Yearnings fhe hath in her own natural kind,
And, even with fomething of a mother's mind,
And no unworthy aim,
The homely nurfe doth all fhe can
To make her fofter-child, her inmate man,
Forget the glories he hath known,
And that imperial palace whence he came.

Behold the child among his new-born bliffes,
A fix years' darling of a pigmy fize !

See, where 'mid work of his own hand he lies,
Fretted by fallies of his mother's kiffes,
With light upon him from his father's eyes !
See at his feet fome little plan or chart,
Some fragment from his dream of human life,
Shaped by himfelf with newly-learned art ;
    A wedding or a feftival,
    A mourning or a funeral;
      And this hath now his heart,
      And unto this he frames his fong :
      Then will he fit his tongue
To dialogues of bufinefs, love, or ftrife ;
      But it will not be long
      Ere this be thrown afide,
      And with new joy and pride
The little actor cons another part ;
Filling from time to time his " humorous ftage "
With all the perfons, down to palfied age,
That life brings with her in her equipage ;
      As if his whole vocation
      Were endlefs imitation.

Thou, whofe exterior femblance doth belie
      Thy foul's immenfity ;
Thou beft philofopher, who yet doft keep
Thy heritage, thou eye among the blind,

That, deaf and filent, read'ft the eternal deep,
Haunted for ever by the eternal mind,—
  Mighty Prophet! Seer bleft!
  On whom thofe truths do reft,
Which we are toiling all our lives to find,
Thou, over whom thy immortality
Broods like the day, a mafter o'er a flave,
A prefence which is not to be put by;
Thou little child, yet glorious in the might
Of heaven-born freedom, on thy being's height,
Why with fuch earneft pains doft thou provoke
The years to bring the inevitable yoke,
Thus blindly with thy bleffednefs at ftrife?
Full foon thy foul fhall have her earthly freight,
And cuftom lie upon thee with a weight,
Heavy as froft, and deep almoft as life!

  O joy! that in our embers
  Is fomething that doth live,
  That Nature yet remembers
  What was fo fugitive!
The thought of our paft years in me doth breed
Perpetual benedictions: not indeed
For that which is moft worthy to be bleft,—
Delight and liberty, the fimple creed
Of childhood, whether bufy or at reft,
With new-fledged hope ftill fluttering in his breaft:—

Not for thefe I raife
The fong of thanks and praife ;
But for thofe obftinate queftionings
Of fenfe and outward things,
Fallings from us, vanifhings ;
Blank mifgivings of a creature
Moving about in worlds not realized,
High inftinɗs, before which our mortal nature
Did tremble like a guilty thing furprifed.
But for thofe firft affeɗions,
Thofe fhadowy recolleɗions,
Which, be they what they may,
Are yet the fountain-light of all our day,
Are yet a mafter-light of all our feeing ;
Uphold us, cherifh, and have power to make
Our noify years feem moments in the being
Of the eternal filence : truths that wake,
To perifh never ;
Which neither liftleffnefs, nor mad endeavour,
Nor man nor boy,
Nor all that is at enmity with joy,
Can utterly abolifh or deftroy !
Hence, in a feafon of calm weather,
Though inland far we be,
Our fouls have fight of that immortal fea
Which brought us hither ;
Can in a moment travel thither,

And fee the children fport upon the fhore,
And hear the mighty waters rolling evermore.

Then fing, ye birds, fing, fing a joyous fong!
    And let the young lambs bound
    As to the tabor's found!
We, in thought, will join your throng,
    Ye that pipe and ye that play,
    Ye that through your hearts to-day
    Feel the gladnefs of the May!
What though the radiance which was once fo bright
Be now for ever taken from my fight,
    Though nothing can bring back the hour
Of fplendour in the grafs, of glory in the flower;
    We will grieve not, rather find
    Strength in what remains behind,
    In the primal fympathy
    Which, having been, muft ever be,
    In the foothing thoughts that fpring
    Out of human fuffering,
    In the faith that looks through death,
In years that bring the philofophic mind.

And, oh ye fountains, meadows, hills, and groves,
Think not of any fevering of our loves!
Yet in my heart of hearts I feel your might;
I only have relinquifhed one delight,

To live beneath your more habitual ſway.
I love the brooks, which down their channels fret,
Even more than when I tripped lightly as they ;
The innocent brightneſs of a new-born day
                    ·   Is lovely yet ;
The clouds that gather round the ſetting ſun
Do take a ſober colouring from an eye
That hath kept watch o'er man's mortality ;
Another race hath been, and other palms are won.
Thanks to the human heart by which we live ;
Thanks to its tenderneſs, its joys, and fears ;
To me the meaneſt flower that blows can give
Thoughts that do often lie too deep for tears.

Printed in Great Britain
by Amazon